how2become

Critical Thinking Tests:

*Understanding Critical
Thinking Skills, and How to
Pass Critical Thinking Tests*

www.How2Become.com

As part of this product you have also received FREE access to online tests that will help you to pass your exams.

To gain access, simply go to:

www.PsychometricTestsOnline.co.uk

Get more products for passing any test at:

www.How2Become.com

Orders: Please contact How2Become Ltd, Suite 14, 50 Churchill Square Business Centre, Kings Hill, Kent ME19 4YU.

You can order through Amazon.co.uk under ISBN: 9781911259374, via the website www.How2Become.com or through Gardners.com.

ISBN: 9781911259374

First published in 2017 by How2Become Ltd.

Typeset by Gemma Butler for How2Become Ltd.

Disclaimer

Every effort has been made to ensure that the information contained within this guide is accurate at the time of publication. How2Become Ltd is not responsible for anyone failing any part of any selection process as a result of the information contained within this guide. How2Become Ltd and their authors cannot accept any responsibility for any errors or omissions within this guide, however caused. No responsibility for loss or damage occasioned by any person acting, or refraining from action, as a result of the material in this publication can be accepted by How2Become Ltd.

The information within this guide does not represent the views of any third-party service or organisation.

CONTENTS

INTRODUCTION

Welcome to *Critical Thinking Tests: Understanding Critical Thinking Skills, and How to Pass Critical Thinking Tests.* In this guide, you'll learn everything that you need to know about critical thinking. From the basics of constructing good arguments, all the way up to different kinds of argumentative fallacy, you'll be fully prepared to take on Critical Thinking assessments.

This book will contain the following:

1. An introduction to the Critical Thinking test, including what it is, why employers use it, and how you can best prepare for it.

2. A primer on what critical thinking is, and why it's such an important skill in the modern working world.

3. Non-Verbal and Inductive Reasoning tests, to prepare your brain for critical thinking.

4. A rundown on the good and bad habits for constructing arguments.

5. In-depth discussion, guidance, explanation, and examples for the five key areas in a Critical Thinking test: inferences, assumptions, deductions, interpretations, and the evaluation of arguments.

6. A sample test for you to use in your Critical Thinking test practice.

What Are Critical Thinking Tests?

The Critical Thinking test is one of many assessments used to evaluate candidates' critical thinking skills. The Critical Thinking test is the most popular means of assessing the critical thinking skills of job applicants.

We'll get onto what exactly critical thinking is, but first it's important to take a quick look at what the test is measuring. Here are the skills that the critical thinking appraisal evaluates:

• The ability to make accurate inferences;

• The ability to identify assumptions being made;

• The ability to make deductions based on text, and then come to conclusions;

• The ability to interpret and evaluate arguments.

Finally, there's no set material that you need to learn for the Critical Thinking test. By this, we mean that you won't need to revise a case study, or enter with prior knowledge of the role you're applying for, in order to pass the Critical Thinking test. The Critical Thinking test only cares about your ability to work with what you're given, in order to come to logical conclusions. Therefore, you'll be given all of the information that you need, in order to answer the question. So, before a Critical Thinking test, all you can study is critical thinking itself.

What Do Critical Thinking Tests Look Like?

Generally, job-related Critical Thinking tests are taken via the internet. If you do have to sit a Critical Thinking test as part of your application, you'll probably face it before any telephone interviews, but only after submitting your CV and application form. The Critical Thinking test will often be part of a larger series of assessments, such as Abstract Reasoning, Numerical Reasoning, or Situational Judgement.

Depending on the kind of Critical Thinking test you take, the time limit and number of questions will differ. Some tests might take 30 minutes – these will usually contain 40 questions. Other forms of the Critical Thinking test might be 60 minutes long, but will contain 80 questions. Either way, this plays out as less than one minute for each question. This means that you have to be quick when answering questions, whilst also paying close attention to them.

While most Critical Thinking tests are taken via the internet, it isn't inconceivable that you will have to sit the test in person, at an assessment centre. The test should be similar to the ones taken online, but be prepared to take more than one Critical Thinking test over the course of application.

How Can I Prepare For Critical Thinking Tests?

The first step in preparing for the Critical Thinking test is to read this book. Here, you'll be given plenty of guidance in becoming a critical thinker, which will allow you to take on any Critical Thinking test. You'll have access to explanations of question types, sample questions and answers, and tips for becoming a better critical thinker. In addition, you can complete the practice test at the end of the book, to see where your strengths lie and where you need to improve.

On top of this, there are a few activities that you can insert into your daily life. One of these is reading non-fiction reports, articles, journals, and editorials. These can be in any topic, from sports to neuroscience; find something that interests you, or an area that you're familiar with, and then start reading pieces from a range of different sources. Focus on the arguments being made in the pieces you're reading, boiling them down into straightforward points.

Let's take a look at an example:

A long-form piece might make the argument that the increasing amount of mass shootings in the USA isn't due to there being more firearms in circulation. Instead, inappropriate media coverage that glorifies the killers increases the chances of a 'copycat killer' emerging. From this, you could potentially generate a simple argument:

Premise 1: Lots of people consume media from various sources.

Premise 2: The media tends to prioritise news involving mass killings, and often goes into detail about the weapons used and background of the killer.

Premise 3: Certain individuals in society might see the attention that these killers get, and decide to do the same themselves.

Conclusion: Therefore, inappropriate coverage of mass shootings in turn causes more similar attacks.

You might be able to find some problems with this argument. For example, it might be difficult to find a causal link between the three premises and the conclusion. While it may be the case that copycat killings are more likely depending on how high-profile the mass shooting is, this might just be a correlation rather than causation. There could be a number of unseen factors which cause the shootings to be more likely.

As a critical thinker, you'll be given the tools to spot these kinds of argumentative flaws. Reading plenty of articles will help you get used to the way arguments are formed, and the shapes they take. Once you've got to grips with logical fallacies, you'll get better at noticing them in text.

Finally, it's beneficial to watch live debates on any issue. If you're studying at university, then there's probably a debating society which will advertise debates that you can attend. If this isn't the case, and there aren't any debates you can attend easily, there are plenty recorded online for you to watch. Better yet, try and get involved in a debating team yourself, so you can hone your argument skills and ability to think critically about what others have to say.

How Should I Use This Book?

The aim of this book is for it to cover everything you need to know in order to pass a Critical Thinking test. From the core tools of logical fallacies, to explanations for each kind of answer, you'll have the knowledge required to complete the Critical Thinking test.

However, your work doesn't end there. Unlike many other tests, where you can just recite core knowledge in order to pass, critical thinking requires you to be able to apply what you've learned. Since you don't know exactly what your questions will be like, you have to be prepared to identify issues within arguments. As previously mentioned, the best way to improve this skill is to use the practice test and sample questions provided, as well as reading plenty of non-fiction work to get used to picking apart arguments.

In the next chapter, we'll take a look at what critical thinking is in more detail. We'll discuss what critical thinking is, why it's such an important skill to have, and why employers love to see it in a candidate.

WHAT IS CRITICAL THINKING?

Have you ever been in a debate with someone about something, and they've said something that sounds dubious? Perhaps they made a claim and failed to provide evidence to support it, or they shot down your argument for reasons that didn't seem relevant. If you picked up on either of these, then you might have an eye (or ear) for critical thinking.

Critical thinking is the activity of studying arguments, the ideas that they're made up of, and the logic that binds them together. When partaking in critical thinking, you're concerned with the structure of arguments, and whether they follow the conventions of argument. If an argument follows these rules, then it's usually considered to be a strong argument. However, if an argument sounds suspicious, imprecise, or poorly supported, then you'll need to figure out why and identify it. This is the role of the critical thinker both during debates and everyday life.

Critical thinkers need to be on the lookout for the following errors made in argument:

- Logical fallacies (e.g. appeals to emotion, appeals to authority);

- Leaps in logic which don't follow from one to another.

Critical thinking is a valuable skill in any walk of life, and is highly valued by employers. This is because having critical thinking skills demonstrates that individuals are committed to looking at situations logically, carefully interpreting evidence, and following arguments to the most well-informed conclusion. This is useful in numerous careers and positions. Essentially, any job that is evidence-based will make good use of critical thinking skills. Therefore, it's in your employer's best interests to ensure that candidates are capable of thinking critically.

Why Is Critical Thinking So Important?

Critical thinking is valuable for a number of reasons, and its exact use to you will depend on your circumstances. For some people, a strong knowledge of critical thinking allows them to construct convincing arguments. After all, if you know what a bad argument looks and sounds like, you'll be able to recognise when your arguments could be stronger, and adjust them adequately. If you wanted to construct a convincing argument for something you believe in, then critical thinking would give you the tools to argue in a way that avoids logical fallacies, whilst also being clear and engaging.

Alternatively, critical thinking can be used to pick holes in arguments and beliefs that other people hold. For example, you might know someone who holds many racial prejudices, whilst using recent terrorist attacks as evidence for why his or her thinking is acceptable. You could argue that he or she is 'cherry-picking' evidence that supports their belief, whilst ignoring data that contradicts his or her claim. Therefore, he or she is making an unfair generalisation.

In the modern age of mass information, thanks to the internet, it's possible to be bombarded by news, facts, and opinions. Sadly, not everyone is so concerned with telling the truth, as they are with pushing ideological agendas or manipulating people for their own financial gain. This means that you can't believe everything that you read. Not only will critical thinking equip you with knowledge about arguments, fallacies, and other argumentative missteps, but becoming a critical thinker involves gearing your brain up in a way that will make you more aware of good and bad argumentation. So, when you read an article in a newspaper or on the internet, you'll be tuned in to all of the little argumentative tricks that the writer is using to compel you to agree with them. This means that critical thinking is an excellent tool for those who want to think for themselves, rather than just believe what they're told.

What this means is that critical thinking can be applicable to everyday life. You can use it to argue your case, find flaws in other people's arguments, and carefully dissect claims made in the media or other places.

Why Do Employers Care About Critical Thinking?

While critical thinking is a great skill to possess in general, some employers also care about candidates being able to demonstrate and use critical thinking skills in a work environment. After all, why else would you be required to take a Critical Thinking test in order to get the job?

Employers like to see critical thinking skills for two reasons:

1. Critical thinking demonstrates high intelligence and self-awareness. Being able to create strong arguments, as well as identify argumentative flaws, is a difficult skill to train properly. Therefore, you need to be intelligent and committed – two traits that employers love to see.

2. Critical thinking is as useful in the workplace as it is in everyday life. In some jobs, critical thinking skills will be necessary to create plans based on evidence, and identify what the problems with current objectives are.

Critical thinking can be used to point out faulty arguments or incorrect ways of thinking that could have a great impact on a business. For example, let's say that you work for a company that's currently doing exceptionally well. Year on year, profits are rising. After three years of this trend, executives might increase bonuses, or expand in ways that would cost a lot of money. Either way, the company will be overspending because they assume that profits will be up once again this year.

This is an example of the 'hot-hand' fallacy – where one assumes that, because they're 'on a roll', they simply can't lose. What if they overspent this year, and then profits happened to fall drastically? Pointing out that they can't be sure that profits will rise, and therefore should exercise caution, could prevent serious damage to the business. Fallacies such as the 'hot-hand' are unknowingly used all the time, even by incredibly intelligent people. Critical thinkers are useful in situations like these because they're more likely to identify flaws in argument and thought processes than those who aren't aware of them.

A critical thinker's mindset has other excellent applications, such as the ability to closely follow a piece of text and highlight issues with it. At school, or perhaps in some job applications, you might have been asked to do a 'comprehension' task. This involves reading a passage, and then answering questions based on it. The goal here is to test the candidate's ability to pick out key pieces of information when answering questions.

Critical thinking is similar to this, as it requires you to pay close attention to a piece of text or spoken argument, and extract the most important details. However, critical thinkers go a step further than simply regurgitating facts – they need to get 'behind' these statements, and find out what conditions they're operating under. Are the statements an inference based on data, or are they baseless assumptions? These are the skills that employers find incredibly useful, which is why you'll be assessed on them in the Critical Thinking test.

How Can I Prepare to Be a Good Critical Thinker?

In order to be an effective critical thinker, you need to adopt a critical thinker's mindset. This involves a number of different activities and lifestyle changes. We've already discussed reading articles and watching debates; on top of those, there are a few things you can do to make yourself a better critical thinker.

Question Your Beliefs

The first step that you can take at any time is to start questioning things you've been told. You don't have to reject everything you know, but take some time to think about the following questions:

1. How do I know that God exists?

2. How do I know that I exist?

3. How do I know that the sun will rise tomorrow?

4. How do I know that the external world that I experience exists?

5. How do I know that the fridge light turns off when I shut the door?

6. How do I know that two plus two equals four?

To think about these beliefs in such a way, is known as scepticism. When thinking about all of the above, you might actually come to reasonable conclusions.

For example, you don't know for certain that the fridge light turns off when the fridge shuts, because you can't observe it. However, you can observe pressing the button inside the fridge which turns off the light. You can also observe the shape of the fridge door, and conclude that when it shuts, the inside of the door presses against the button, which turns off the light. Therefore, you can be sure that the fridge light turns off when you shut the door.

For other questions, the answer might not come as easily. For instance, the only way you might 'know' that the sun will rise tomorrow is because it's risen every day since the earth came into being. However, just because it's risen every day *so far*, that doesn't guarantee that it must rise tomorrow. This is a form of inductive argument – a generalisation based on previous observations. You might argue that the sun rising every day is a rule or law of nature, but how do we know this? For all we can tell, it may just be the case that the sun rising every day is a regularity, something that happens every day by chance.

In response to this, one might suggest that while we cannot know for certain that the sun will rise tomorrow, the fact that it has risen for every day in history gives us good reason to. In other words, it's technically *likely* that the sun will rise tomorrow, even if we don't know it will for certain.

It isn't a problem if you don't have adequate answers to these questions. Philosophers have been puzzled by these same topics for thousands of years, so don't feel as though you need to have all of the answers. What's important here is the ability to question your beliefs, and get to the heart of why you might believe them. We believe that the sun will rise tomorrow because it always has done. We believe that the external world around us exists because maybe it's a simpler explanation than everything being an illusion.

It's also fine to accept some of these core beliefs, even if they don't always hold up to this kind of scrutiny. Extreme scepticism is an incredibly difficult position to maintain whilst also living one's everyday life, so don't worry about rejecting every belief you've ever held. What's more important is your ability to think critically about what you think you know.

Read Some Philosophy

Although reading non-fiction of all kinds is helpful when trying to become a critical thinker, reading philosophy can put you a step further. You don't need to cover everything, or even read whole books, but try and expose yourself to philosophical arguments and how they're presented. If you can't seem to get into the original works, try and find some companion books or other secondary sources written about the initial book. This will give you the arguments in a format that's easier to understand.

Conclusion

Now you have an idea about what critical thinking is, and why it's such an important skill to have. As previously mentioned, being a good critical thinker requires having a specific mindset, carefully attuned to noticing things that others might not. In the next chapter, you'll have the opportunity to prepare your brain for critical thinking with some

Inductive and Non-Verbal Reasoning questions.

PREPARING
YOUR BRAIN FOR
CRITICAL THINKING

In this chapter, we'll take a look at Abstract and Inductive Reasoning. The reason for this is that both involve identifying and understanding patterns and detail – a vital skill for a critical thinker. Use these questions to get your brain in gear for critical thinking.

Abstract Reasoning Questions

Question 1

Which set does the test shape belong to?

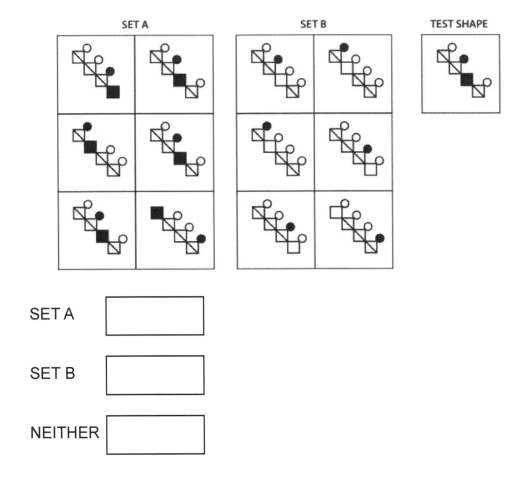

SET A

SET B

NEITHER

Question 2

Which set does the test shape belong to?

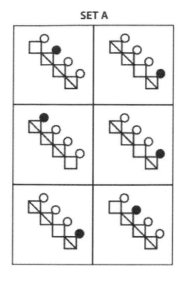

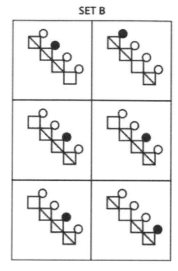

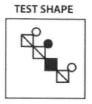

SET A   SET B   TEST SHAPE

SET A ☐

SET B ☐

NEITHER ☐

Question 3

Which set does the test shape belong to?

SET A   SET B   TEST SHAPE

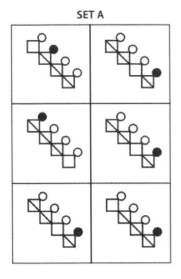

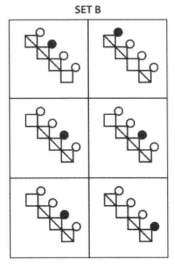

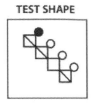

SET A   [   ]

SET B   [   ]

NEITHER   [   ]

Question 4

Which set does the test shape belong to?

SET A   SET B   TEST SHAPE

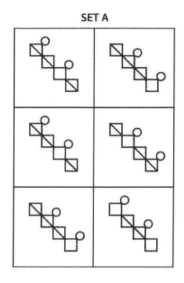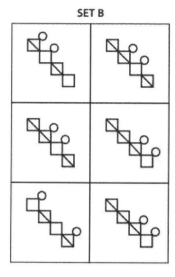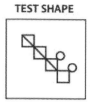

SET A

SET B

NEITHER

Question 5

Which set does the test shape belong to?

SET A   SET B   TEST SHAPE

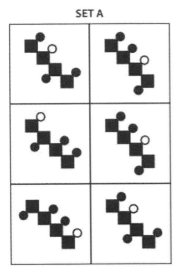
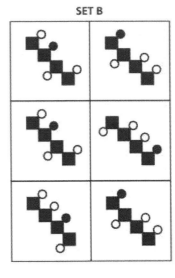
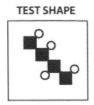

SET A [   ]

SET B [   ]

NEITHER [   ]

Question 6

Which set does the test shape belong to?

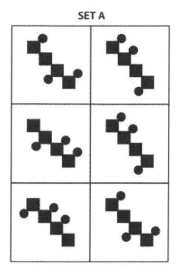

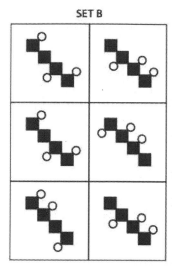

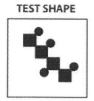

SET A

SET B

NEITHER

Question 7

Which set does the test shape belong to?

SET A   SET B   TEST SHAPE

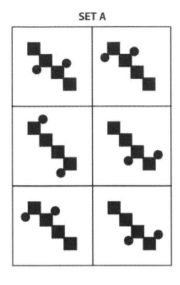 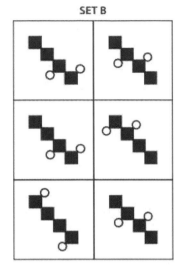 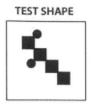

SET A

SET B

NEITHER

Question 8

Which set does the test shape belong to?

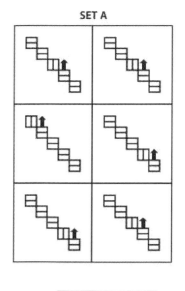

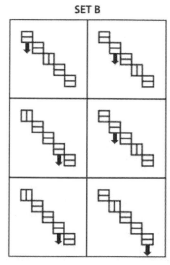

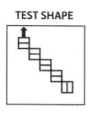

SET A

SET B

TEST SHAPE

SET A ☐

SET B ☐

NEITHER ☐

Question 9

Which set does the test shape belong to?

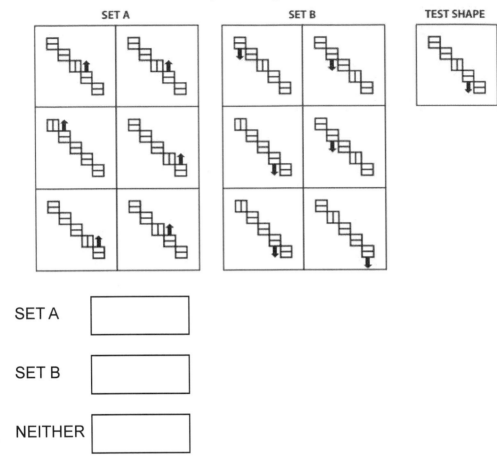

SET A   ☐

SET B   ☐

NEITHER   ☐

Question 10

Which set does the test shape belong to?

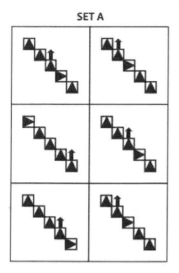

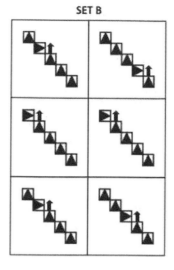

SET A

SET B

TEST SHAPE

SET A [   ]

SET B [   ]

NEITHER [   ]

Inductive Reasoning Questions

Question 1

Which of the following is the odd one out?

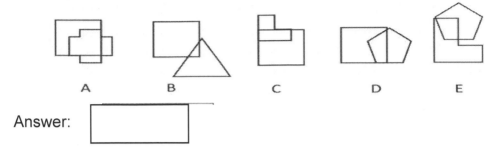

Answer: [   ]

Question 2

What comes next in the sequence?

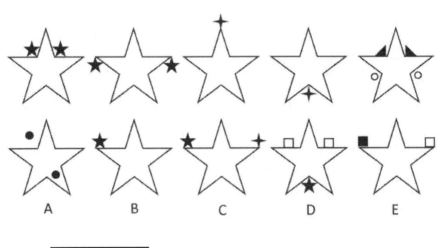

Answer: [   ]

Question 3

Which answer fits in the sequence?

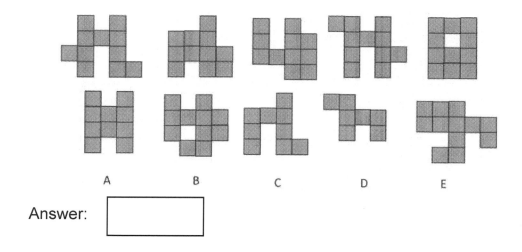

Answer:

Question 4

What comes next in the sequence?

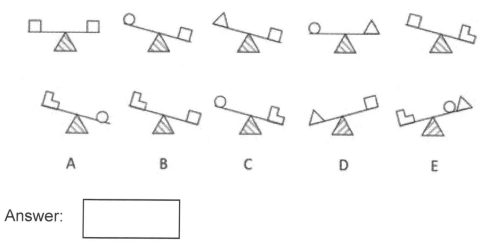

Answer:

Question 5

What comes next in the sequence?

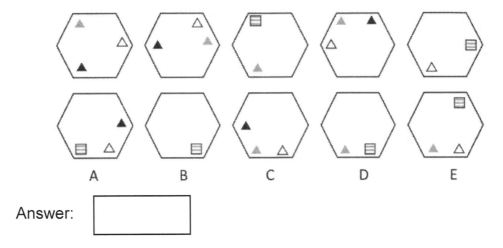

A   B   C   D   E

Answer:

Question 6

What comes next in the sequence?

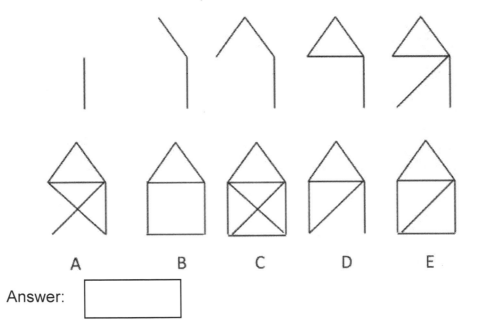

A   B   C   D   E

Answer:

Question 7

Which answer fits in the sequence?

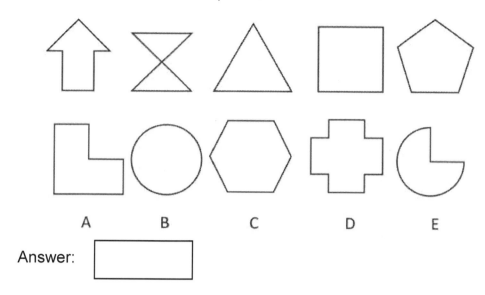

A B C D E

Answer:

Question 8

What comes next in the sequence?

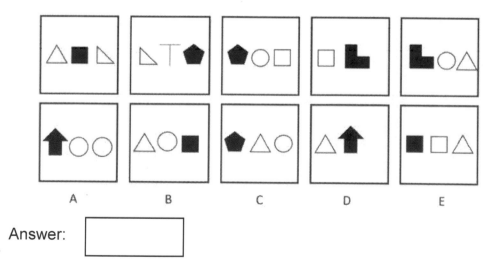

A B C D E

Answer:

Question 9

Which answer fits in the sequence?

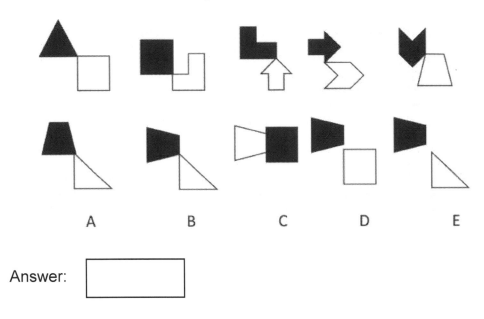

A   B   C   D   E

Answer: [   ]

Question 10

What comes next in the sequence?

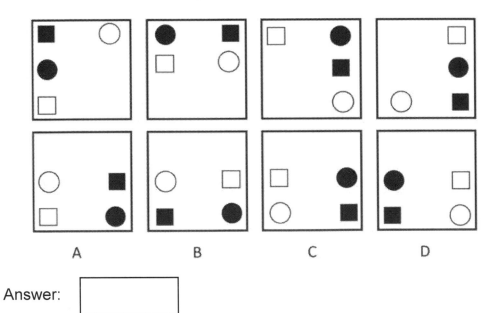

A   B   C   D

Answer: [   ]

Abstract Reasoning Answers

Q1. SET A

The Test Shape fits with Set A because it has 2 white dots and 1 black dot. It also has one black square and 3 squares that have diagonal lines.

SET A: There are 4 squares in a diagonal. If a square has a black dot, then the following square down in the sequence is black and does not have a dot. If the last square in the sequence of 4 has a black dot, the first square will be black.

SET B: There are 4 squares in a diagonal. If a square has a black dot, then the following square down in the sequence does not have a line running through it. If the last square in the sequence of 4 has a black dot, the first square will be the one without the line running through it.

Q2. NEITHER

The Test Shape doesn't fit in to either. It is clear that both sets do not contain a black square and the Test Shape does, therefore doesn't belong to any set.

SET A: There are 4 squares in a diagonal. If a square has no line running through it, then the next square down has a black dot. If the last square in the sequence of 4 has no line running through it, then the first square will have a black dot.

SET B: There are 4 squares in a diagonal. If a square has no line running through it, then the second square down from it will have a black dot. If the last square in the sequence of 4 has no line running through it, then the second square from the top will have a black dot.

Q3. SET B

The Test Shape fits with Set B because the black dot is two spaces in front of the square that has no line running through it, which follows the pattern of Set B.

SET A: There are 4 squares in a diagonal. If a square has no line running through it, then the next square down has a black dot. If the last square in the sequence of 4 has no line running through it, then the first square will have a black dot.

SET B: There are 4 squares in a diagonal. If a square has no line running through it, then the second square down from it will have a black dot. If the second from last square in the sequence of 4 has no line running through it, then the first square from the top will have a black dot.

Q4. SET B

The Test Shape fits with Set B because if the square has a diagonal line running through it and a white dot, the next square will have a white dot but no diagonal line in the square. The Test Shape follows this pattern.

SET A: There are 4 squares in a diagonal. If a square has a line running through it and a white dot, then second square down from it also has a white dot but no line running through it. If the last square in the sequence of 4 is the one with a line running through it and a white dot, then the second square from the top with have a dot but no line running through it.

SET B: There are 4 squares in a diagonal. If a square has a line running through it and a white dot, then the next one down from it also has a white dot but no line running through it. If the last square in the sequence of 4 is the one with a line running through it and a white dot, then the first square at the top will have a dot but no line running through it.

Q5. NEITHER

The Test Shape doesn't fit in to either Set. In Set A, it contains 3 black dots and only one white. Set B contains 3 white dots and only 1 black. The Test Shape has 4 white dots, so therefore cannot fit in to either Set.

SET A: There are 4 black squares in a diagonal. If a square has a white dot located in the top right hand corner, then the next square down from it will have a black dot on the bottom left hand corner. If the last square in the sequence of 4 is the one with a white dot, then the first square at the top of the sequence will be the one with a black dot on the bottom left hand corner.

SET B: There are 4 black squares in a diagonal. If a square has a black dot located in the top right hand corner, then the next square down from it will have a white dot on the bottom left hand corner. If the last square in the sequence of 4 is the one with a black dot, then the first square at the top of the sequence will be the one with a white dot on the bottom left hand corner.

Q6. NEITHER

The Test Shape doesn't fit in to either Set. In Set A, it contains 3 black dots. In Set B, it contains 3 white dots. The Test Shape contains 4 black dots and therefore cannot fit in to either Set.

SET A: There are 4 black squares in a diagonal. If a square has no dot located on the top right hand corner, then the next square down from it will have a black dot on the bottom left hand corner. If the last square in the sequence of 4 is the one with no dot, then the first square at the top of the sequence will be the one with a black dot on the bottom left hand corner.

SET B: There are 4 black squares in a diagonal. If a square has no dot located on the top right hand corner, then the next square down from it will have a white dot on the bottom left hand corner. If the last square in the sequence of 4 is the one with no dot, then the first square at the top of the sequence will be the one with a white dot on the bottom left hand corner.

Q7. NEITHER

The Test Shape doesn't fit in to either Set. In Set A, If a shaded square has a dot on the bottom left corner, then the next shaded square will have a dot on the top right corner. In Set B, the same thing is happening as seen in Set A, except they are white dots instead of black. The Test Shape shows if the square has a dot on the top right corner, then the next square will have a dot on the bottom left corner.

SET A: There are 4 black squares in a diagonal. If a square has a black dot located on the bottom left hand corner, then the next square down from it will have a black dot on the top right hand corner. If the last square in the sequence of 4 is the one with a black dot on the bottom left hand corner, then the first square at the top of the sequence will be the one with a black dot on the right-hand corner.

SET B: There are 4 black squares in a diagonal. If a square has a white dot located on the bottom left hand corner, then the next square down from it will have a white dot on the top right hand corner. If the last square in the sequence of 4 is the one with a white dot in the bottom left hand corner, then the first square at the top of the sequence will be the one with a white dot in the right-hand corner.

Q8. SET A

The Test Shape fits with Set A. The first vertical square in the sequence means the next square will have an arrow pointing upwards. In the Test Shape, the vertical square is the last in the sequence, so the arrow will be placed at the start of the sequence.

SET A: There are 5 white squares in a diagonal. If a square has a vertical line running through it, then the next square will have a black arrow pointing upwards. If the last square in the sequence of 5 is the one with a vertical line running through it, then the first square at the top of the sequence will be the one with an arrow pointing upwards.

SET B: There are 5 white squares in a diagonal. If a square has an arrow pointing downwards, then the second square that follows in the sequence will have a vertical line running through it. If the second to last square in the sequence of 5 is the one with an arrow pointing downwards, then the first square at the top of the sequence will be the one with a vertical line running through it.

Q9. NEITHER

The Test Shape doesn't fit in to either Set. It cannot fit in to Set A because the arrows are pointing up and in the Test Shape, they are pointing down. In Set B, there are four consecutive squares that have horizontal lines, the arrow is placed on the third square. However, the Test Shape places the arrow on the first square that has a horizontal line.

SET A: There are 5 white squares in a diagonal. If a square has a vertical line running through it, then the next square will have a black arrow pointing upwards. If the last square in the sequence of 5 is the one with a vertical line running through it, then the first square at the top of the sequence will be the one with an arrow pointing upwards.

SET B: There are 5 white squares in a diagonal. If a square has an arrow pointing downwards, then the second square that follows in the sequence will have a vertical line running through it. If the second to last square in the sequence of 5 is the one with an arrow pointing downwards, then the first square at the top of the sequence will be the one with a vertical line running through it.

Q10. SET B

The Test Shape fits with Set B. If the triangle in the square is pointing to the right, then the next square will have an arrow pointing upwards. It cannot fit into Set A because the arrow is placed above the square that has the triangle pointing to the right.

SET A: There are 5 white squares in a diagonal. If a square has an arrow standing on top of it, then the next square in the sequence will have a triangle pointing to the right inside it. If the last square in the sequence of 5 is an arrow standing on top of it, then the first square in the sequence will be the one with a triangle pointing to the right inside it.

SET B: There are 5 white squares in a diagonal. If a square has a triangle pointing to the right inside it, then the next square in the sequence will have an arrow standing on top of it. If the last square in the sequence of 5 is the one a triangle pointing to the right inside it, then the first square in the sequence will be the one with an arrow standing on top of it.

Inductive Reasoning Answers

Q1. E

Rule 1 = each figure must contain a square.

Figure E is the odd one out because all of the other figures contain a square, whereas Figure E does not follow this rule and therefore makes it the odd one out.

Q2. D

Rule 1 = there must be at least one line of symmetry through the figure.

Figure A can be ruled out because it has no lines of symmetry. Figure B can be ruled out because it has no lines of symmetry. Figure C can be ruled out because the black star on the left would not reflect the black star on the right. Figure E can be ruled out because the black square on the left would not reflect the white square on the right.

Q3. B

Rule 1 = the pattern needs to include 11 squares.

Figure A can be ruled out because it only contains 10 squares. Figure

C can be ruled out because it only contains 9 squares. Figure D can be ruled out because it only contains 7 squares. Figure E can be ruled out because it contains 12 squares.

Q4. C

Rule 1 = squares weigh more than the circles.

Rule 2 = squares weigh more than the triangles.

Rule 3 = triangles and circles weigh the same.

Rule 4 = 'L' shapes weigh more than the squares.

Figure A can be ruled out because the 'L' shape weighs more than circles. Therefore, the scales are not correct. Figure B can be ruled out because the 'L' shape weighs more than squares; therefore, the scales are incorrect. Figure D can be ruled out because squares weigh more than triangles. Figure E can be ruled out because you are not given any indication as to whether the circle and the triangle would weigh more than the 'L' shape.

Q5. D

Rule 1 = the grey triangle moves around the points of the hexagon two places clockwise.

Rule 2 = the white triangle moves around the points of the hexagon one place anti-clockwise.

Rule 3 = the black triangle moves around the points of the hexagon one place clockwise.

Rule 4 = if any of the shapes coincide and end up at the same point, the shapes automatically become a patterned square.

Figure A can be ruled out because the white triangle should be a striped rectangle, and the striped rectangle should be a grey triangle. Figure B can be ruled out because a grey triangle needs to be placed in the bottom left corner of the hexagon, and a black triangle needs to be placed in the middle right corner of the hexagon. Figure C can be ruled out because none of the smaller shapes are in the correct position. Figure E can be ruled out because the striped rectangle should be in the bottom right corner (replacing the white triangle), and a black triangle needs to be added to the middle right corner of the hexagon.

Q6. D

Rule 1 = you need to draw the figure without the pen leaving the paper.

Rule 2 = you cannot go over any line more than once.

Figure A can be ruled out because the next line drawn will be a vertical line to form the left side of the house. Figure B can be ruled out because a diagonal line has disappeared and instead has drawn in the rest of the outer house. Figure C can be ruled out because your next figure will still have 2 lines missing. Figure E can be ruled out because you cannot draw both the bottom line of the house and the left vertical line.

Q7. C

Rule 1 = an extra line of symmetry is added as the sequence progresses.

Figure A can be ruled out because this has no lines of symmetry. Figure B can be ruled out because a circle is symmetrical no matter what way you rotate it. Figure D can be ruled out because this shape has 4 lines of symmetry; we need a shape with 6 lines of symmetry. Figure E can be ruled out because this only has 1 line of symmetry.

Q8. D

Rule 1 = the first shape in each of the figures, must be the same as the last shape in the previous box.

Rule 2 = the shape with the most number of sides is black.

Rule 3 = all the sides of each shape in the figure must add up to 10.

Figure A can be ruled out because the sides only add up to 9. Figure B can be ruled out because the sides only add up to 8. Figure C can be ruled out because the sides only add up to 9. Figure E can be ruled out because the sides add up to 11. Also, the shape with the most sides is a square. However, there are two squares in this figure, so both squares should be black.

Q9. B

Rule 1 = the white shape at the end of the figure, becomes a black figure at the start of the next figure.

Rule 2 = the white shape is also rotated 90° clockwise to form the first shape of the next figure.

Rule 3 = both shapes need to be joined at one of the points of each shape.

Figure A can be ruled out because the black shape has not been rotated 90° clockwise (from the previous figure). Figure C can be ruled out because the trapezoid should be black. Also, the shapes need to be joined at points from both shapes. Figure D can be ruled out because the shapes are not joining by the points of both shapes. Figure E can be ruled out because the shapes are not joining by the points of both shapes.

Q10. B

Rule 1 = the shapes move round one place clockwise in each figure.

Figure A can be ruled out because the two squares are in the wrong place; the black square should be where the white square is; and the white square should be where the black square is. Figure C can be ruled out because this is a horizontal reflection of answer option A. Figure D can be ruled out because this is a vertical reflection of answer option C.

THE ETIQUETTE OF ARGUMENT

So far, we've taken a look at the following:

- What critical thinking is;

- What the Critical Thinking test is;

- Abstract and Inductive Reasoning questions to get your brain ready for critical thinking.

In this chapter, we're going to be taking a look at how arguments work. Since critical thinking is mostly focused on identifying, examining, and dissecting arguments, knowing the rules and conventions for argumentation is vital for passing the Critical Thinking test.

Everything that you learn in this chapter will be useful in the Critical Thinking test. In particular, the rules and conventions will be helpful for the 'evaluating arguments' questions found in the assessment. This type of question examines your ability to identify strong and weak arguments. In this chapter, you'll find out what kind of qualities make for strong arguments, as well as the errors which can be found in weak arguments.

These conventions will also be useful for other kinds of question. For example, a lot of fallacies made in arguments are assumptions of some kind. This could prove useful when it comes to identifying assumptions in the assumption questions of the Critical Thinking test.

Likewise, leaps in logic are a core part of the deduction and interpretation sections of the Critical Thinking test. Needless to say, unwarranted leaps in logic aren't preferable when making an argument, so they will be covered here.

In a more general sense, learning how to argue effectively can be useful in your everyday life. You'll be able to identify poor arguments that others make, as well as strengthen your own position while in a debate.

The Rules of Structuring an Argument

Like almost any discipline, there are rules and conventions when it comes to forming arguments. These conventions have been built upon over centuries of philosophical, political, mathematical, and scientific debate. This means that they vary, from queries about the very structure of an argument, all the way to manipulation of statistics to enforce one's own agenda.

Generally speaking, an argument takes the form of one or more **premises**, followed by a **conclusion**. In a sense, the premises are the foundation of an argument, whilst the conclusion is built from it. This means that, if the premises aren't strong, then one might question the strength of the conclusion. Likewise, if the conclusion does not fit the premises (or the conclusion does not **follow** from the premises), then the argument will also be questionable.

Here's an example of a syllogism, one of the most common types of logical argument:

> Today is Thursday. It will rain between Wednesday and Friday. Therefore, it will rain today.

This is a kind of logical deduction, which involves two premises and a conclusion. It can be re-written as the following:

> **Premise 1:** Today is Thursday.
>
> **Premise 2:** It will rain between Wednesday and Friday.
>
> **Conclusion:** It will rain today.

All arguments are built from premises and a conclusion. In this case, we have a logical deduction – the conclusion is derived from the two premises and confined to the information given in the premises.

There are other kinds of argument too, such as inductions. These are the result of premises and a conclusion, but usually contain a generalisation of some kind. For example:

> **Premise 1:** Every time I go outside, I get stung by a wasp.
>
> **Conclusion:** Therefore, I'll get stung by a wasp next time I go outside.

Inductive arguments assume regularity in events. Here's another inductive argument:

> **Premise 1:** There has never been a day where the sun hasn't risen.
>
> **Conclusion:** Therefore, the sun will rise tomorrow.

Both of these arguments assume that, based on previous occurrences, that the same things will occur again. However, there is no guarantee of this, even if it may seem likely. So, while it's likely that the sun will rise tomorrow, it isn't inevitable.

As you can see, arguments are bound together by rules and conventions. The majority of the rules that we'll be looking at in this chapter fall under the category of fallacies. These take many different forms, so it's important to read each of them carefully.

What Are Fallacies?

There are a few different definitions of a fallacy, such as:

1. A false belief based on questionable arguments.

2. Faulty reasoning.

While these are slightly different definitions, they both touch on the idea of poor reasoning. In essence, this is what a fallacy is – a case of reasoning which is considered faulty.

Fallacies can appear in a number of different situations. Sometimes, the speaker does not realise that they've committed a logical fallacy, and has no intention of deceiving people or subverting reason. In other cases, fallacies are purposefully made to convince people of a position that would be untenable on purely rational grounds. In either case, fallacies need to be identified in order to prevent irrational arguments from being made, or potentially incorrect conclusions from being accepted as a fact.

The issue with fallacies is that, despite not pertaining to reason, they can still be incredibly convincing, especially to those who cannot identify them. This is one of the reasons why critical thinkers are valued by employers – they can spot unsound reasoning where others might not. This is vital in some lines of work, such as law and economics, but applies to almost any career where important decisions need to be made.

Whenever a decision needs to be made, there will likely be conflicting opinions regarding the course of action to take. Naturally, this tends to lead to debate. Two or more parties will present their arguments, discuss them, ask questions about each other's position, and hopefully arrive at the best conclusion based on reason and evidence.

However, things don't always go so smoothly. Some people have an aversion to being proven incorrect, and this can result in fallacies being made to make sure that others agree with them. Sometimes, an individual has an agenda that they want to push forward. If this agenda isn't rational, then irrational means might be necessary in order to convince people that it is the correct action to take.

Whatever the case, good critical thinking skills can make the difference between a strong argument being picked as the better one, or a weaker position being forwarded. This can be crucial in some businesses, and is also useful in everyday life.

Fallacies mostly fall under two major categories:

1. **Formal logical fallacies** – an argument with an invalid logical form.

2. **Informal logical fallacies** – an argument which may have a valid logical form, but the premises of the argument do not adequately support the conclusion.

A formal logical fallacy is one in which the conclusion does not necessarily follow from the premises, which are assumed to be correct for the sake of argument. If the leap from premise to conclusion does not follow, then a formal logical fallacy has been committed.

In contrast, an informal logical fallacy occurs when a conclusion may follow from the premises, but the truth or falsehood of the premises themselves is disputable. Therefore, the *premises* of an argument are often the focus when it comes to identifying informal fallacies.

While both forms of fallacy are important for critical thinking, it's likely that only informal logical fallacies will appear in the Critical Thinking test. For this reason, we're going to focus on them.

Informal Logical Fallacies

As previously mentioned, informal logical fallacies are less concerned with the *structure* of the argument made, and are more focused on its *content*.

Informal logical fallacies are most likely to appear in the 'evaluating arguments' section of the Critical Thinking test, where you'll be asked to identify which arguments are strong, and which are weak. One of the most important factors when evaluating an argument's strength is whether it contains logical fallacies or not. While the inclusion of an informal logical fallacy in an argument doesn't make it invalid by default, fallacies usually indicate a weaker argument.

The main issue with informal logical fallacies is that, to the uninitiated, they can be incredibly convincing. However, anyone with a grasp on critical thinking and reason should be able to identify and reject fallacious arguments.

Informal fallacies are usually divided into the following categories:

- Fallacies of relevance – this occurs when the evidence provided in the premises of an argument are irrelevant to the conclusion;

- Fallacies of weak induction – the evidence given isn't strong enough to lead to the conclusion;

- Fallacies of ambiguity – the conclusion relies on evidence which isn't present **or** evidence is manipulated either deliberately or accidentally in order to reach the conclusion.

Let's take a look at the most common informal fallacies in these three categories.

Fallacies of Relevance

Fallacies of relevance occur when the speaker uses irrelevant evidence in their argument. This can be used in order to get to their conclusion, or to undermine their opponent's argument. For example, *ad hominem* is a fallacy of relevance because it's a personal attack. No matter what the circumstances of the individual making an argument are, what should be attacked is the argument – not the person making it.

The following fallacies are among the most common fallacies of relevance that you'll find in the Critical Thinking test, as well as in everyday life.

Ad Hominem

This argument is also known as 'personal attack' or 'argument against the person'. Simply put, this fallacy occurs when the speaker makes comments about their opponent, or uses their opponent's circumstances in order to strengthen their own claim or undermine their opponents. Take a look at the following example:

> 'My opponent knows nothing about the NHS and how it works – he grew up wealthy and has had private healthcare all his life!'

This argument is fallacious, because it presumes that the speaker's opponent cannot know anything about the NHS because they use private healthcare. This might be the case, but isn't necessarily true. For example, the opponent might be a high-ranking NHS doctor, or a government official who is quite knowledgeable about the NHS. So, the circumstances of the individual don't elucidate how strong the argument is.

Moreover, *ad hominem* is fallacious because it doesn't examine the merits of the argument. Consider the following:

Say that an incredibly rich person makes the argument that the NHS is faulty and needs to be replaced with a new system. The response that their opponent might make is that, because the speaker is rich, they haven't experienced what it means to need the NHS. This, of course, is *ad hominem*.

However, what if the exact same argument was made – but instead of a rich speaker, it was a working-class individual who relied on the NHS for healthcare. The argument is the same, but now this *ad hominem* would no longer apply. This is one of the easiest ways to spot a fallacy of this kind.

Ad hominem is one of the most straightforward fallacies to identify with and deal with. Remember that, if an argument attacks the individual rather than the opponent's argument, then it is fallacious. Generally speaking, these arguments are weak.

Appeal to Authority

This fallacy is somewhat similar to *ad hominem*, in that it uses an individual's circumstances to strengthen one's position. However, in this case it's the reverse – finding a position of authority to support your argument.

For example, let's say that you're locked in a debate and trying to argue in favour of belief in God. The following would be a fallacious argument:

> 'Belief in God isn't absurd, because plenty of intelligent people have also believed in God. Isaac Newton, Charles Darwin, and Albert Einstein all believed in some kind of god. Therefore, we should believe in God.'

This is an appeal to authority, because it uses the example of famous intellectuals in order to support one's own argument. The argument made above assumes that, because Newton, Darwin, and Einstein were intelligent pioneers in Science, they must be correct when it comes to belief in God. However, just because they were intelligent people, this does not mean that they were right about everything.

Here's another example of an appeal to authority:

> 'I know best when it comes to matters about the NHS. I am a doctor, after all.'

This is an appeal to authority, because the speaker is using their own position of authority in order to strengthen their position. Essentially, the speaker is asking the audience to trust whatever they have to say, simply because they're in a position of authority.

This kind of fallacy is usually employed when the individual making the argument needs to convince the audience of something, but lacks evidence. To mask this logical leap, the speaker uses their position of authority to speak for itself.

Of course, being an authority on a matter doesn't hurt your argument. Being an authority gives you access to information that others might not have. Authority should be used to get better evidence, rather than used in place of evidence.

Appeals to authority also take the form of irrelevant quotations. Sometimes, a speaker might pull a quote from a famous or likeable individual in order to support their argument, rather than hard evidence.

Appeals to authority are fairly obvious to spot, because they will refer to someone who is held in high regard, or someone who you can apparently trust.

Appeal to False Authority

Appeal to false authority is similar to a regular appeal to authority, but the 'authority' being relied on is dubious or unreliable. For example, if someone cited a lawyer who had been disbarred in their argument, this could be considered a false authority.

This can also occur when individuals whose expertise is irrelevant to an argument is cited. For example, if someone cites their favourite musician as an authority when it comes to why you should vote for a specific political party, then this is an appeal to false authority. While this musician might be incredibly talented in their own field, their endorsement of a political party doesn't serve as a strong argument on its own.

Appeal to Emotion

Appeal to emotion is an attempt to evoke an emotional response from the opponent or the audience, rather than give evidence for their argument. Take note that it's completely acceptable for an argument to evoke emotion – this is unavoidable in most controversial issues – but the argument cannot *rely* on emotion in order to convince the audience or undermine the opponent.

The following is an example of an appeal to emotion:

> 'I find it disgusting that there are still people living rough in the UK, don't you?'

The aim of the above question is to put the opponent in a difficult position. If they agree, then they might be compromising their own argument. However, if they disagree, they might come across as callous or even cruel. In a debate with an audience, this could be used to sway the audience in the speaker's favour, rather than convince them by using reason.

This is a fallacy of relevance, because the emotions of the speaker, opponent and audience are not a valid replacement for evidence and reasoning. The emotional response of any of these parties is irrelevant.

Appeal to emotion is usually easy to identify. If the argument includes emotive language, or questions the emotional status of the audience or opponent, then it is appealing to emotions rather than making a strong argument.

Appeal to Nature

The appeal to nature is a particularly common fallacy employed when discussing what is right or wrong. An appeal to nature is made when the speaker assumes that something that is natural is necessarily good, correct, or moral. Conversely, the same fallacy is made if one assumes that something that is unnatural is bad, incorrect, or immoral.

Here's an example of an appeal to nature:

> 'Genetically-modified crops could be a risk to people's health – all those chemicals and modified DNA must be harmful.'

This argument assumes that, because genetically-modified crops aren't natural, they must be a threat to people's health. However, there are plenty of things which could be considered natural that are bad.

For example, the venom from a poisonous snake is natural, and it's also natural for the snake to bite prey or potential predators. However, we wouldn't say that it's good to be bitten by a snake, or that it's good that the snake injects venomous poison into its victims. We might not say it's bad or wrong either. The status of it being natural has no impact on whether we think that it's good, correct, or moral.

This argument is sometimes portrayed as 'playing God', especially when it comes to ethical issues such as genetic modification and embryonic screening.

Argument from Incredulity

This fallacy is an appeal to the incredulity of a claim. Essentially, the speaker summarises a point of view, and then comments on how that sounds implausible or unlikely. This can be either personal incredulity, or general incredulity. Here's an example of personal incredulity:

> 'A floating man in the sky who listens to our prayers? That sounds unlikely to me.'

This is a fallacy because what you personally *feel* about the likelihood of something is irrelevant to the discussion. Your intuitions about how likely something is could be false. Rather, you should be using statistical data which alludes to how likely something is.

This fallacy can be identified by the speaker making reference to how probable they believe something to be, without sufficient evidence.

Bandwagon Fallacy

This is also referred to as the appeal to popularity or *ad populum*. Fallacies of this kind will make the claim that, since a large group of people do or believe something, then it must be true. Take a look at the following example:

> 'Over a billion people are now connected to social media websites. Can it really be so bad?'

The issue with this fallacy is that it makes the assumption that, because so many people believe in something, then it can't be wrong. However, we know that this isn't the case. For example, until Nicolaus Copernicus published *On the Revolutions of the Celestial Spheres*, the consensus was that the earth existed at the centre of the universe, and everything else rotated around it. Whether they were intelligent or not, rich or poor, almost everyone in the world would accept that the earth was the centre of the cosmos. However, after the Copernican Revolution happened, this changed.

The central premise of the bandwagon fallacy is that so many people can't all be wrong. However, in the case of Copernicus' findings, it was the case that almost everyone was incorrect. Therefore, no matter how many people believe something to be true, this alone does not guarantee its truth.

This is a fallacy of relevance because the number of people who believe in something does not serve as evidence. It can easily be identified by the speaker making reference to how many or few people agree with them.

'Fallacy' Fallacy

This fallacy is one which assumes that, because the opponent's argument is fallacious, the conclusion they reach must be incorrect. This is a fallacy because the commitment of a fallacy does not mean that the position you're defending is automatically false. Instead, it just means that the argument presented to defend the position is insufficient.

Here's an example of a 'fallacy' fallacy:

> 'You argue that producing genetically-modified foods is immoral because it will lead us on a slippery slope to genetically-modified humans. This is a fallacy. Therefore, it is moral to produce genetically-modified foods.'

This is a fallacy because the position itself is independent of the speaker arguing for it. It might be the case that a position is incredibly defensible, but has had the misfortune of poor speakers defending it. Therefore, a fallacious argument does not invalidate a position – it merely demonstrates that the argument itself is weak.

Fallacies of Weak Induction

Fallacies of weak induction are those which, while offering some kind of relevant evidence, use evidence which isn't sufficient to lead to the desired conclusion. This can also include spurious generalisations.

Anecdotal Evidence

Anecdotal evidence is evidence that the speaker has sourced from personal experience. Here's an example of anecdotal evidence:

> 'I'm yet to meet someone who doesn't think that this is ridiculous.'

In this claim, the speaker is implying that, because they haven't met someone who disagrees on this issue, most people must agree on this issue.

Anecdotal evidence is fallacious because the sample of people that the speaker is fielding isn't necessarily representative of the population. For example, let's say that you're arguing in favour of increasing education on voting and politics. If you made the following argument, you'd be committing the anecdotal evidence fallacy:

> 'Everyone I know who doesn't vote say that they would if they knew more about the political parties running in elections. Therefore, we need to improve politics and current affairs education.'

The problem with this argument is that the sample of the population you're using to support your argument, might not reflect the entire country. It might be the case that most people who don't vote choose not to because they simply don't care. Your sample of the population isn't representative for two reasons:

1. It's probably too small (polls and surveys gather evidence from thousands of people).

2. The demographic is probably quite specific, since you're asking people you've met. This probably means that the people you've asked share a lot of the same interests, have similar beliefs, or come from around the same area (unless stated otherwise, polls and surveys gather data from a wide range of demographics).

So, this is a fallacy of weak induction because you're making an inductive argument (a generalisation), based on unreliable data. It's fairly easy to identify, since it's usually telegraphed by phrases such as 'from my experience'.

Here's another example of an argument based on anecdotal evidence:

> 'I've never seen a black swan. Therefore, there is no such thing as a black swan.'

This is anecdotal, since you're basing the inductive argument on your own experience. It might just be the case that you've never been to a place where there are black swans. Therefore, you can't ignore the possibility that black swans exist.

Cherry-Picking/Texas Sharpshooter

This fallacy involves the speaker only picking data which supports their argument, and ignoring evidence which might refute their claim. This is an issue because the speaker's argument isn't being founded on sturdy evidence. When doing critical thinking, one should aim to push the argument which is most well-supported by evidence, data, and reasoning.

This fallacy can be tricky to spot because the speaker usually only displays the evidence that supports their claim. In the Critical Thinking test, compare the data being cited in the arguments compared to the data in the passage.

For example, a passage says that unemployment is down but homelessness is up. Then, an argument says that we should continue supporting the current government because unemployment is down, and therefore people are better off. This argument is deliberately ignoring data which doesn't support it. Therefore, it is committing the cherry-picking fallacy.

Correlation Proves Causation

This is a statistical fallacy which assumes that, because there's a correlation between two phenomena, one must be causing the other. For example:

> 'In almost every case, babies grow hair before they grow teeth. Therefore, growth of hair causes teeth to grow.'

Here, the speaker is correctly recognising a correlation. Generally speaking, babies do grow hair before they grow teeth. However, to say that one causes the other is inaccurate. We can re-write this argument as follows:

> Babies grow hair = Phenomenon A
>
> Babies grow teeth = Phenomenon B
>
> Phenomenon A happens in every case that phenomenon B happens.
>
> Phenomenon A occurs before phenomenon B.
>
> Therefore, phenomenon A is the cause of phenomenon B.

This argument overlooks the possibility that there's a cause for both of these phenomena, which explains why there's a correlation between the two. In this case, it's the natural process of growth, which is phenomenon C. This means that, rather than *A causes B*, *C causes A and B*.

Even if there isn't a clear third cause, it's important not to jump to the conclusion that there's a causal relationship between two or more phenomena. Instead, there might be a hidden third phenomena which is causing both.

It might even be the case that there is no third cause, and that the correlation is freakish coincidence. This is less likely, but still a reason not to assume a causal relationship between two phenomena.

Whenever an argument makes uses of data in order to reach a conclusion, keep an eye out for what conclusion they're making. If the causal link they're suggesting could be explained by another cause, then they might be committing a false cause fallacy.

Argument from Ignorance

This is the assumption that a claim is true, because it is yet to be proven false, or cannot be proven false. Likewise, it is the assumption that a claim is false because it is yet to be proven true, or cannot be proven to be true.

Take a look at the following two examples:

> 'There's no evidence to show that God exists. Therefore, God does not exist.'

> 'There's no evidence to show that God does not exist. Therefore, God exists.'

This is a fallacy because, just because we don't currently have the evidence to show that something is true or false, this does not automatically mean it is either true or false.

Argument from Silence

An argument from silence is one which reaches a conclusion because there's no evidence against it, rather than evidence to support it. This is a fallacy because, even if there's no evidence that something *isn't* the case, that doesn't automatically mean it is the case. When making a claim, it is vital that you substantiate it. Evidence to refute your claim is only necessary once you've given evidence for your own position.

This is somewhat similar to the burden of proof, where the speaker assumes that their opponent has to provide evidence to prove them wrong, before the speaker has given data to substantiate their own claim.

Here's an example of an argument from silence:

> 'There's no evidence to show that we **do** possess free will. Therefore, we **do not** possess free will.'

Burden of Proof

Technically, the burden of proof is not a fallacy in itself. The burden of proof is a principle that states that whomever is making a claim needs to substantiate it with evidence. It is not the job of the opponent to provide evidence against a claim.

The burden of proof is used fallaciously when the speaker making a claim insists that their opponent proves them wrong. This is similar to the arguments from silence and ignorance, but focuses more on the opponent's ability to present a counter-argument to an unsubstantiated claim being made by the speaker.

This is often used fallaciously when the speaker cannot give evidence of their position, but they also know that their opponent cannot give evidence to refute it.

Here's an example of the burden of proof being used fallaciously:

> 'I might not be able to prove that God **does** exist, but can you prove that he **doesn't**?'

When making a claim, it is always the responsibility of the claimant to substantiate their argument with evidence. Until then, the opponent does not have to prove them wrong.

Gambler's Fallacy

The gambler's fallacy is a statistical fallacy which assumes that statistically independent occurrences somehow affect one another. For example, one might believe that they are 'due a win' after a series of losses at a roulette table. However, the amount of times that you've lost at the roulette table doesn't make it more likely that you will win on the next try, since the outcome of one spin doesn't have any effect on the next.

A slightly related fallacy to this is the Hot hand fallacy, where one believes that the person participating in the seemingly random activity can have an effect on the outcome. For example, if you were performing poorly on the roulette table, but your friend was on a winning streak, one might think you'd be better giving your chips to her. However, your friend is no more likely to win than you are – they aren't naturally gifted at winning a completely random game.

No True Scotsman

This fallacy is one which involves moving the goalposts in order to make evidence against one's position invalid. The best way to demonstrate this is with an example:

> John claimed that no Scotsmen drink wine. Brian, who is a Scotsman, says that he drinks wine. John replies by saying that no **true** Scotsman would drink wine.

The purpose of this fallacy is to combat legitimate evidence against one's argument by changing the conditions for the evidence. In this quintessential case, John says that 'no *true* Scotsman' would drink wine. However, since no one could agree on what a 'true' Scotsman is, John could exclude any evidence that refutes his argument. This is sometimes referred to as a *self-sealing* argument since it is unfalsifiable. What we mean by unfalsifiable is that, due to the way the argument is formulated, it is impossible to provide evidence against it.

Generally speaking, an argument will not be taken seriously if there is no way of proving it wrong. Creating a self-sealing argument is a way of making your argument unfalsifiable, and therefore is considered to be a fallacious reasoning.

Slippery Slope

The slippery slope is one of the most common fallacies that you'll see in debate, and it's also one of the easiest to identify.

A slippery slope is committed when the speaker assumes that the first relatively small step will inevitably lead to a catastrophic or otherwise undesirable one.

Here's an example of a slippery slope:

> 'If we promote genetically-modified foods, what's next? Genetically-modified people?'

This is a fallacy, because the speaker has no way of demonstrating that producing genetically-modified foods will inevitably lead to genetic engineering. Therefore, this is a fallacy of weak induction. In some cases, this can be considered as an argument from fear, as the speaker might claim that a seemingly harmless step will lead to a terrifying one.

Slippery slopes are usually easy to identify. Sometimes, the speaker even refers to them as 'slippery slopes' in their own argument – which makes them even easier to spot.

A slope is acceptable if the speaker is able to give evidence for *Event A* leading to *Event B*. However, to claim that this is a definite progression from *A* to *B* isn't reasonable, since you can't prove that future events will definitely happen.

Fallacies of Ambiguity

A fallacy of ambiguity is a case of faulty reasoning, where the speaker has made content of the argument ambiguous. This can include confusing the meanings of words, using an unclear definition to jump to a conclusion, or misrepresentation of arguments.

Argument to Moderation

An argument to moderation is a fallacy which states that the compromised 'middle-ground' between two viewpoints is the correct one by default. While it's quite common for the best answer to exist between two extremes, the problem here is that some people will make the leap to the conclusion that the middle ground is always the best one.

Here's an example of an argument to moderation:

> James believed that tuition fees for students should remain at £9,000 per year. Ishmael argued that tuition fees should be scrapped entirely, and that a 'graduation tax' should be implemented. Ryan stepped in and highlighted a compromise – that tuition fees should remain at £9,000 **and** a graduate tax should be implemented.

Sometimes, a compromise isn't the best answer. The assumption that this fallacy makes is that an extreme viewpoint cannot be correct, and therefore needs to be watered down to suit the middle. Likewise, this kind of argument guesses that the middle ground will suit everyone. However, in the above example, both parties would be unsatisfied with the compromise.

So, while compromise can be a legitimate third-way during debate, the assumption that the middle ground is best by default is fallacious.

Begging the Question

Question begging is a form of fallacious reasoning that requires one to accept the conclusion of an argument in order to accept either one or more of its premises. In essence, this means that the premises are dependent on the conclusion, rather than the other way around.

In an argument, the premises should serve as a foundation for the conclusion to rest on. In a valid deductive argument, this means that if both premises are true, then the conclusion must also be true. The conclusion follows from two premises which are independent from it.

An argument which begs the question is different. Instead, the conclusion is required to be accepted as truth, in order for one of the premises to be true.

The following is an extremely common argument which begs the question.

Premise 1: The Bible says that God exists.

Premise 2: The Bible can be trusted, since it was written by God.

Conclusion: Therefore, God exists.

This argument begs the question in its second premise. Premise 2 argues that the Bible is trustworthy because it was written by God. However, in order to accept this, one must accept that God exists. After all, if God does not exist, then he could not have written the Bible. However, in order to accept premise 2, you have to believe that God exists. Therefore, premise 2 relies on the truth of the conclusion in order for itself to be true. Therefore, it is begging the question.

Question begging is a form of circular reasoning, because the argument relies on itself in order to be true, rather than having premises which exist independently of the conclusion. Therefore, it is fallacious.

False Dichotomy

A false dichotomy is a fallacy which assumes that there are only two possible positions in a debate, when in fact there may be more. A quintessential example of this type of fallacy is the phrase 'if you aren't with us, you're against us.' When making this fallacy, the speaker assumes that there are only two positions – both of which are starkly contrasted.

While this might sometimes be the case, the vast majority of debates and issues are more complex than black and white, or good and evil.

It's perfectly acceptable for there to be a position which agrees with elements of both sides, or even has nothing in common with either. This argument is a simplification of what could be incredibly complex issues. In turn, this can lead to a straw man argument – where the speaker misinterprets their opponent's view (usually making it look more extreme than it really is).

Here's an example of a false dichotomy:

> 'So, if you're not in favour of scrapping tuition fees, you must think that they are acceptable as they are.'

This is fallacious, because it fails to acknowledge that the opponent might be against the end of tuition fees, but isn't happy with them at their current level. The opponent might not want to remove tuition fees, but instead simply wants to reduce them. This is fallacious, because it assumes what the opponent's position is, without considering the possibility of subtlety.

In a sense, the false dichotomy is the opposite of an argument to moderation. Rather than assuming that the middle ground is always best, the false dichotomy assumes that there is no tenable middle ground *at all*.

False Equivalence

False equivalence is a fallacy that makes a comparison between two cases, when in fact the comparison is impossible to make. This can be because the two cases are different in kind (colloquially referred to as being 'apples and oranges'), and in other cases they are so different in scale that a comparison is tenuous at best.

Here's an example of a false equivalence between two cases that are different in kind:

> 'Some Muslim women conceal their faces in public. Criminals also try to conceal their faces when committing crimes. Therefore, Muslim women are as dangerous as criminals.'

This is a false equivalence in kind, because these two parties conceal their faces for fundamentally different reasons. Muslim women conceal their faces for cultural and religious reasons. Criminals try to hide their faces in order to avoid being identified by witnesses or the police. Therefore, while this might seem to be a legitimate equivalence on the surface, it doesn't hold up under scrutiny.

Here's an example of a false equivalence between two cases that are different in scale:

> 'What with the existence of diversity quotas to fulfil, being a white man in the job market is like being a Jewish person in Nazi Germany.'

The implication here is that white men in the current jobs market are essentially persecuted for their gender and ethnicity, since diversity quotas might mean that companies look instead for women and people from ethnic minorities. In this case, the comparison is made to Jews in Nazi Germany, who were forced into ghettos, worked to death, or killed en masse. While it might be the case that white men are being discriminated against due to the existence of diversity quotas, this comparison isn't acceptable because the difference in severity is too large to be accurate.

This argument is fallacious because it tries to conflate two incomparable cases in order to make a point. This can be used in combination with an appeal to emotion by using emotionally-charged comparisons, such as the Holocaust.

The best way to identify this kind of fallacy in the Critical Thinking test is to look at the two cases being compared. If they are different in kind or severity, then the argument is likely committing this fallacy.

Single Cause Fallacy

The single cause fallacy is a form of faulty reasoning that oversimplifies causation, so that a phenomenon has either very few or one cause. This is fallacious because it's usually impossible to know exactly how many things are responsible for something to occur. In addition to this, there are lots of causes which might not be easily recognisable, or are so far-removed from the phenomenon that no one thinks to include them.

In other cases, a number of possible causes are identifiable, but the speaker explicitly rejects all but one of them.

Here's an example of a single cause fallacy:

After a school shooting, several different groups demanded for change to prevent another from happening. Some argued that more gun control was necessary, whilst others believed that the issue was to do with how the media glamorises mass murderers. Others opted to blame the parents, whilst the rest believed that the current schooling system was a breeding ground for teenage angst and eventual violence.

This is an example of a single cause fallacy, because each of these groups believed that only one of these factors was the cause of the school shooting, when in fact all of these might have played a role. Often, the causes of an event are much more complicated than any single phenomenon. Therefore, it is fallacious to assume that there can only be one cause for a phenomenon.

Straw Man

The straw man is an extremely common form of argument in modern discourse – perhaps somewhat due to people's tendency on social media to only read headlines rather than full articles.

To 'put up a straw man' is to misrepresent your opponent's argument, whether intentionally or not. This can involve oversimplification in order to make the opponent's argument easier to attack, or making the argument look more extreme than it actually is.

Here's an example of a straw man fallacy:

Jeff believes that the prison system should focus on rehabilitation of convicts rather than merely punishing them. He argues that, at least in some cases, criminals should be allowed to work whilst serving their sentences, in order to give them the skills they need to reintegrate with society once they've served their sentence. This would be dealt with on a case-by-case basis, and these criminals would not be allowed to work in an environment which required a DBS check – such as working with children.

Jeff's opponent, Andrew, says the following:

'Jeff wants to let murderers back into work, where they could be a threat to society!'

This is a misrepresentation of Jeff's argument, since he specifically mentions that this would be dealt with on a case-by-case basis. It's implied from Jeff's argument that those convicted of more extreme crimes, such as murder, would not get this opportunity. Therefore, Andrew is attempting to misrepresent Jeff's argument to make it easier to attack.

Conclusion

You now have the necessary tools to identify strong and weak arguments, which will prove useful throughout the Critical Thinking test and everyday life. In particular, you'll be able to make use of what you've learned here for the 'evaluating arguments' questions in the test. For the next few chapters, we'll be taking a look at the different kinds of question that you'll face in the Critical Thinking test.

CRITICAL THINKING
– INFERENCES

For the next five chapters, we're going to focus on the types of question you might find in the Critical Thinking test. You should expect all five of these types to appear in your test, due to the fact that you'll have many questions to answer. The five types of question are:

- Inferences;

- Assumptions;

- Deductions;

- Interpretations;

- Evaluation of arguments.

All of these will appear in a Critical Thinking test. Therefore, it's vital that you prepare for them.

In these chapters, we'll go through each of these five areas, step-by-step. We'll begin with an explanation of what they are in more general terms, then focus on how to recognise and answer questions about them. Finally, we'll supply some sample questions for you to answer, in order for you to familiarise yourself with the type of question. Let's start with inferences.

What Are Inferences?

When someone infers something, or makes an inference, then they are coming to a conclusion which is based on evidence. Logic (whether inductive or deductive) is applied to this evidence, which in turn brings the individual to their conclusion. When someone makes an inference, they're commonly seen as 'reading between the lines', figuring out a conclusion that isn't explicit, but rather implied from the evidence.

Unlike some of the other types of claim, such as assumptions, inferences are based on evidence. However, inferences aren't always correct, and shouldn't be accepted as truth. While an inference might seem correct, it's entirely possible that it's overlooking other factors relevant to the issue.

It might even be the case that you have plenty of evidence for something, but you completely misconstrue it. All of the evidence going into the inference could be strong, but the way you think about it could be incorrect.

For example, you might come across a police officer talking to an individual in the street. You might infer from the fact that the individual isn't in handcuffs, and that the officer is talking to them, that they witnessed or are reporting a crime. This seems to be a sensible conclusion, but there are other possibilities. The individual might know the police officer personally, and is quickly stopping to say hello to them. Alternatively, they might be asking for directions. So, the inference might be incorrect.

In the Critical Thinking test, you'll be commenting on how *likely* the inferences are to be true or false, rather than if they are simply correct or incorrect. This means that you need to think about all of the other possibilities other than the inference in question. Generally speaking, the more possibilities there are, the less likely the inference is to be true.

However, some inferences are better than others. For example, say that you couldn't find your keys and phone. You were sure that you left them on the kitchen table, but now they're gone. You could make several inferences as to how this happened:

1. A burglar snuck into your house undetected and stole them.

2. There was a brief lapse in the laws of the universe and they disappeared into thin air.

3. A ghost took them to play a practical joke on you.

4. Someone else in your house moved them.

5. You are mistaken about where you left your keys and phone, and they're actually somewhere else.

Some of these inferences are more likely than others. For example, you might say that **inference 1** is probably false. This is because it *could* have happened – it isn't impossible – but the chances of it happening are slim. **Inferences 2** and **3** are, depending on your perspective, either probably false or certainly false. This is because you might consider both of these things to be impossible.

Inferences 4 and **5** will fall into the category of probably true. This is because they are the most rational explanations for why your keys and phone appear to have moved from the kitchen table. They don't rely on the supernatural or incredibly unlikely (perhaps even impossible) changes to the fabric of the universe. Whatever the case, they're far more likely to occur than the first three inferences. Therefore, it might be safe to say that these inferences are probably true, and the most likely overall.

You also need to pay attention to whether or not the inference contradicts the information in the text. For example, say that the text says that people who frequently use social media are more likely to struggle to make friends in 'real life'. If one of the inferences says that social media users are more likely to have more friends, then there's a contradiction between the two. This means that the inference is either probably false, or certainly false.

What Are Inference Questions Like?

In the Critical Thinking test, inference questions are usually formulated as follows. First, you'll be presented with a piece of text about a particular subject. You do not need to know anything about the topic that the passage is focused on – everything you need to work with will be available to you.

Along with the text, there will be three inferences based on it. For each of these inferences, you will need to mark them as one of the following:

Definitely True – Given all of the information in the passage, it is certainly the case that this inference is correct.

Probably True – Given all of the information in the passage, it is likely that the inference is correct. However, it is not guaranteed.

Insufficient data to say whether it is true or false – Given all of the information in the passage, it is impossible to say whether the inference is true or false.

Probably False – Given all of the information in the passage, it is likely that the inference is incorrect. However, this is not guaranteed.

Definitely False – Given all of the information in the passage, it is impossible for the inference to be correct.

So, an inference question will look something like the following:

> Scientific studies have discovered a link between chewing gum and better performance when it comes to tests. Researchers believe that this is because the act of chewing gum correlates with heightened activity in the hippocampus – the region of the brain which handles memory. When activity in the hippocampus is increased, it appears as though the ability to recall memories is strengthened.

Inference 1: Chewing gum causes heightened activity in the hippocampus.

Inference 2: There is a correlation between chewing gum and better recollection of memories.

Inference 3: Students who chew gum will perform worse in exams than students who do not.

Let's take a look at each of these in more detail:

Definitely True

This means that the inference is certainly correct. This inference has no other competing possibilities to contend with, and is a deduction based on the information in the passage. For example, if the text said that coffee drinkers tended to have a higher IQ than those who do not drink coffee, then it's definitely true to say that those who do not drink coffee tend to have a lower IQ than those who do. In other words, this tends to be a **tautology**.

TAUTOLOGY: A STATEMENT THAT IS TRUE OUT OF NECESSITY OR DUE TO ITS LOGICAL STRUCTURE. OR, A STATEMENT THAT'S TRUE BY DEFINITION.

Probably True

This means that the inference is quite likely to be correct, or is more likely to be correct than incorrect. This means that the inference does not contradict the information in the passage in any way. However, the inference may still be incorrect, as other unseen possibilities might be better. For example, if you had quite a few drinks on a night out and had a headache in the morning, it's probably true that the alcohol has given you a hangover. You come to this conclusion by observing the evidence (i.e. 'you had quite a few drinks last night', and 'you have a headache now'), and combining it with an established fact: 'drinking too much alcohol has been known to cause headaches'.

While this makes sense, it isn't guaranteed to be true since there could be other explanations. For example, it might not have been the alcohol that gave you a headache. While on your night out, you might've hit your head while walking down some stairs, but don't remember it too well. It's less likely that you hit your head than the alcohol giving you a headache. Therefore, the hangover explanation is a better inference to be made from the evidence.

Insufficient Data to Say Whether It Is True or False

This answer is most accurate when the inference is irrelevant, or is not supported by the passage. For example, the text might say that coffee drinkers tend to have a higher IQ than those who do not drink coffee. Then, one of the inferences was 'those who drink tea are more likely to have a higher IQ than those who do not drink tea.' If there was no mention of this in the passage, then it's impossible to know whether this inference is true or false. Therefore, the inference is unsupported.

There are other cases where this answer might be acceptable, such as when an inference tries to draw a causal relationship from a correlation. Say that the passage says that coffee drinkers tend to have a higher IQ than non-coffee drinkers. One of the inferences might say 'coffee makes people smarter.' However, based on the evidence in the passage, there's not much reason to believe than there's a causal link between the two. There's certainly a correlation, but this doesn't mean that there's any causation involved. There could be another explanation, such as those with a higher IQ are more likely to want to drink coffee. There's insufficient evidence of a causal relationship for either of these inferences.

While there's no real evidence to support this inference, there's nothing which refutes it, either. Therefore, the correct answer is that there's insufficient data to say whether it is true or false.

Probably False

This answer is correct when the inference seems to contradict the passage, but isn't *necessarily* a contradiction. For example, if the passage stated that coffee drinkers were more likely to have a higher IQ than non-coffee drinkers, but also stated that coffee drinkers tended to have higher blood pressure than non-coffee drinkers, the following inference would probably be false:

'Coffee drinkers tend to be healthier than non-coffee drinkers.'

This is probably false, because higher blood pressure usually indicates worse health. So, if coffee drinkers tend to have higher blood pressure than non-coffee drinkers, it's *likely* that they're less healthy. However, there may be other factors to take into account, such as their immune system or susceptibility to other illnesses. Essentially, while the claim is *probably* false, there isn't quite enough information to say that it is *definitely* false.

Definitely False

An inference is definitely false if it directly contradicts the information in the passage. For example, if the passage says that coffee drinkers tend to have a higher IQ than non-coffee drinkers, then the following inference is definitely false:

'Coffee drinkers have a lower IQ than non-coffee drinkers.'

This directly contradicts information in the passage. Therefore, it's definitely false.

As you can see, each of these types of inference are distinct from one another. The best way to learn how to answer questions properly in this type of question is to read and answer practice questions. However, there are a few other tricks you can employ in order to read between the lines more effectively.

Reading Between the Lines

The key to understanding inference questions is to think about what inferences are more likely to be false than true. Sometimes, this might not be easily quantifiable – you probably won't have access to exact probabilities – so you need to think about what seems most likely. Here are some general rules for each inference:

Definitely True – If the inference directly follows from the passage, and there are no other reasonable alternatives, then this inference is definitely true.

Probably True – If the inference seems to follow from the passage, but might not be conclusively verifiable based on the information in the text, then it is probably true. Think about whether the inference is more likely to be true than false, and is supported by the passage.

Insufficient Data to Say Whether It Is True or False – If there is not enough information to make an educated claim to the inference being true or false, then this answer is correct. This also applies to cases where the inference might be committing a 'correlation/causation' fallacy, or if the inference is completely irrelevant.

Probably False – If the inference is more likely false than true, but does not explicitly contradict the information in the passage, then it's probably false. This means that the inference appears to contradict the statement, but it's still somewhat possible that the inference is true.

Definitely False – If the inference directly contradicts information in the passage, then it is definitely false. As a general rule, if it's impossible for the information in the passage and the inference to both be correct, then the inference is definitely false.

Quite often, the inferences being made will indirectly reference the information in the text. For example, the passage says that 'coffee drinkers tend to have a higher IQ than non-coffee drinkers.' One of the inferences might say 'there is a correlation between people who drink coffee and higher intelligence.' At the very least, this inference is probably true – it follows from the information in the passage. You might even want to say it's definitely true, although this would require accepting that IQ is an accurate representation of one's intelligence.

Either way, it's important to think carefully about what's been written, both in the initial passage as well as the inferences, since there might be a slight difference in terminology that could throw you off.

Inferences – Sample Questions

Now that you've learned what inference questions look like, and how they should be answered, it's time to look at some examples. Try to answer these questions for yourself without checking the answers. If you're struggling with a question, make a note of it and move onto the next one. Answers and explanations will be provided at the end of this chapter, so you can figure out where you've done well, and where you need to improve.

Note: the contents and statistics used in the questions here are used for testing purposes only. The facts and statistics portrayed in these questions are not necessarily true.

Question 1.

In 2015, surveys suggested that the number of polyamorous relationships in the UK had risen by 15% since the previous survey in 2014, meaning that there were approximately 5 million adults in the UK participating in polyamorous relationships. However, the number of monogamous relationships had also increased by 20%.

Inference 1:	In general, more people were in relationships in 2015 than in 2014.
Inference 2:	The rise in polyamorous relationships is causing a decline in monogamous relationships.
Inference 3:	People like polyamorous relationships.

Question 2.

Over the past five years, the number of university students on the electoral roll has decreased by 10% each year. This is despite the fact that the number of students enrolling in politics and foreign affairs courses has increased by 50% over the past five years.

Inference 1:	Everyone who studies politics and foreign affairs is on the electoral roll.
Inference 2:	More people are on the electoral roll than the number who study politics and foreign affairs.
Inference 3:	The rise in students studying politics and foreign affairs is inspiring more students to register to vote.

Question 3.

In an interview, a famous British actor said she believed that the UK government has an obligation to do more for refugees fleeing from areas of crisis. The current government has made no concerted effort to help refugees beyond the bare minimum. This actor says that aiding refugees is one of her top priorities.

Inference 1:	This actor will not be voting for the party currently in power in the upcoming election.
Inference 2:	The opposition has said that they will help refugees if their party is elected.
Inference 3:	The current government is ignoring the refugee problem.

Question 4.

In 2013, tax avoidance in the UK reached the highest it has been in 25 years. According to the statistics, most of this avoidance occurs in the higher tax brackets. Tax in these brackets is higher than it has been in at least the last ten years.

Inference 1:	People are avoiding tax because they are being taxed too heavily in those brackets.
Inference 2:	The number of people avoiding tax will continue to rise.
Inference 3:	There are people avoiding tax in lower tax brackets as well.

Question 5.

A study in October found that approximately 55% of people in poverty in the UK are also in work. By 2020, this figure is expected to rise to 60%. 25% of people in poverty are not in work because they aren't fit to, either due to old age or disability.

Inference 1:	20% of people in poverty are not in work but they are fit to work.
Inference 2:	The number of people in poverty and in work will rise.
Inference 3:	55% of the population is in poverty.

Inferences – Answers

Here are the answers to the inference sample questions:

Question 1

Inference 1: In general, more people were in relationships in 2015 than in 2014.

Answer: Definitely True.

Explanation: The number of both polyamorous and monogamous relationships has increased. Since these are the main two kinds of intimate relationship, it's extremely likely that the number of people in relationships has increased.

Inference 2: The rise in polyamorous relationships is causing a decline in monogamous relationships.

Answer: Definitely False.

Explanation: Monogamous relationships have increased in number. Therefore, the rise in polyamorous relationships isn't causing a decrease in monogamous relationships.

Inference 3: People like polyamorous relationships.

Answer: Probably True.

Explanation: We can't be sure how many people like the polyamorous relationships that they are in. However, it is probably the case that at least *some* people in polyamorous relationships like them.

Question 2

Inference 1: Everyone who studies politics and foreign affairs is on the electoral roll.

Answer: Insufficient data to say whether it is true or false.

Explanation: There's no way to tell from the data in the passage that everyone who studies politics and foreign affairs is on the electoral roll.

Inference 2: More people are on the electoral roll than the number who study politics and foreign affairs.

Answer: Probably True.

Explanation: This inference does not specify the demographic in question. Therefore, it is likely that, across the country, there are more people on the electoral roll than those who study politics and foreign affairs.

Inference 3: The rise in students studying politics and foreign affairs is inspiring more students to register to vote.

Answer: Definitely False.

Explanation: The number of students on the electoral roll is decreasing each year.

Question 3

Inference 1: This actor will not be voting for the party currently in power in the upcoming election.

Answer: Probably True.

Explanation: This actor says that the refugee issue is one of her top priorities. Since the government has had made no effort to increase aid to refugees, it's probably the case that this actor will not be voting for them in the upcoming election.

Inference 2: The opposition has said that they will help refugees if the party is elected.

Answer: Insufficient data to say whether it is true or false.

Explanation: There's no mention of the opposition party in this passage, so we don't know enough to tell whether this claim is true or false. It might be the case that both major parties have no intention of helping refugees.

Inference 3: The current government is ignoring the refugee problem.

Answer: Definitely False.

Explanation: The passage states that the government is doing no more than the *bare minimum*. This suggests that, while aid is poor, the government isn't ignoring the problem. No matter how inconsequential, something is being done.

Question 4

Inference 1: People are avoiding tax because they are being taxed too heavily in those brackets.

Answer: Probably True.

Explanation: While we can't be certain about this, it's fairly safe to assume that the reason why people are avoiding tax is because they're being taxed too highly. There doesn't seem to be any other motive for avoiding tax.

Inference 2: The number of people avoiding tax will continue to rise.

Answer: Insufficient data to say whether it is true or false.

Explanation: Based on the information in the passage, we don't know what will happen to these tax brackets in the future. Therefore, we can't tell whether the number of people avoiding tax will increase or not.

Inference 3: There are people avoiding tax in lower tax brackets as well.

Answer: Definitely True.

Explanation: The passage says that 'most' of this tax avoidance is occurring in the higher tax brackets. This means that people in lower tax brackets are avoiding tax as well.

Question 5

Inference 1: 20% of people in poverty are not in work but they are fit to work.

Answer: Definitely True.

Explanation: 55% of people in poverty are in work. 25% of people in poverty aren't in work but also aren't fit to work. This leaves 20% left over for people in poverty, not in work, but fit to work.

Inference 2: The number of people in poverty and in work will rise.

Answer: Probably True.

Explanation: The passage claims that by 2020 the number of people in poverty and in work is expected to rise. This doesn't guarantee that it will happen, but seems likely.

Inference 3: 55% of the population is in poverty.

Answer: Insufficient data to say whether it is true or false.

Explanation: The passage says that 55% of the impoverished population is in work. It says nothing about how much of the overall population is in poverty.

CRITICAL THINKING – ASSUMPTIONS

In this chapter, we're going to be looking at assumptions – what they are, how to identify them, and how to approach them during the Critical Thinking test.

What Are Assumptions?

An assumption is a claim that is accepted as the truth without sufficient evidence. These are an issue for critical thinkers because, as a rule, claims made without factual evidence are unhelpful and can be misleading. For example, imagine if you worked at a company, and the success and survival of it depended on a continued market demand for DVDs. If, at the start of each financial year, executives at the company agreed that DVDs would continue to sell based on zero evidence, this would be an assumption. This could be dangerous since the sales of DVDs could suddenly drop, leaving the company in a difficult position. For this reason, it's important to avoid making assumptions in the working world.

Assumptions are made quite often when constructing arguments. You might have heard the phrase, 'for the sake of the argument, let's assume that...' This is an explicit example of an assumption being made – an assumption that is required in order for the argument to make sense. In other words, you shouldn't leave anything up to assumption when making an argument – even if all parties agree on the truth of the assumption.

What Are Assumption Questions Like?

As previously mentioned, people use assumptions when they're making a claim or constructing an argument. Sometimes, the person making the argument is explicit about their assumptions: 'Let's assume that...' These assumptions are obviously easiest to spot, and can be contested if one feels that the assumptions are incorrect.

However, some assumptions aren't as identifiable. Sometimes, the person constructing the argument won't make their assumptions explicit. For the most part, this is down to one of the following reasons:

a) The person making the argument knows that this assumption is incorrect, and is deliberately trying to conceal it to make their argument look stronger.

b) The person making the argument doesn't even realise that their argument is based on the assumptions that they've subconsciously made.

In either case, it's important in a critical discussion to highlight assumptions, whether they're correct or not.

> **Explicit Assumption:** An assumption made during construction of an argument, which is disclosed by the person making the argument.
>
> **Implicit Assumption:** An assumption which is not disclosed by the person making an argument.

Assumption questions in the Critical Thinking test assess your ability to highlight what assumptions an argument or statement is making. For questions of this kind, you'll be given a statement, usually followed by three assumptions. Take a look at this example:

'If I go down to the pond today, the only birds I will see are swans.'

Assumption 1: There will be no ducks at the pond.

Assumption 2: All swans are white.

Assumption 3: There will be swans at the pond today.

Your task is to identify which of the above assumptions, if any, are being made by the text. In other words, you need to state whether the assumption is being made ('Assumption Made') or if the assumption isn't being made by the argument ('Assumption Not Made'). These assumptions are implicit, so you need to spot them for yourself. Take a look at the following answers and explanations to the above example:

Assumption 1: There will be no ducks at the pond.

Answer: Assumption Made.

Explanation: In order to only see swans at the pond, there must be no other birds. Since ducks are a kind of bird, their presence at the point would mean you'd see them as well as swans. Therefore, there cannot be any ducks at the pond in order to only see swans.

Assumption 2: All swans are white.

Answer: Assumption Not Made.

Explanation: The statement does not specify what colour the swans have to be, only that swans have to be seen. Therefore, this assumption is not implied by the statement.

Assumption 3: There will be swans at the pond today.

Answer: Assumption Made.

Explanation: This is an assumption made by the initial statement because in order to see swans at the pond, there must be swans at the pond.

Assumption questions are more straightforward than inferences, because you don't need to worry about probability. All you need to do is see if the argument relies on any of the assumptions in order to be correct. If the argument requires the assumption, that means it's an assumption being made by the text ('Assumption Made'). If the argument doesn't require the assumption, then it isn't an assumption being made by the text ('Assumption Not Made').

Assumptions Versus Presumptions

People often use the terms 'assume' and 'presume' interchangeably. One might say 'I presume there will be space in the car park' *or* 'I assume there will be space in the car park.' While many people will use both terms as though they are equivalent, there's a slight difference between the two that's moderately useful when constructing an argument or participating in a debate.

The difference between the two is one of strength, rather than core meaning. They both mean the same thing: to take something for granted, or accept something as truth with little evidence. However, a presumption is usually more authoritative, implying that there's at least some evidence to support the claim.

Another interpretation of the two words depends on when they're being used. If you believe something before it occurs, you are making a presumption about it. For example, 'I presume that the weather will be nice tomorrow' is a presumption because you're making a statement about the future. The word assumption is acceptable in this situation, as well.

However, the term 'presumption' is unsuitable when discussing something that's happened, or is currently happening. For example,

'I assume he made it to the train station in time' is correct, whilst 'I presume he made it to the station in time' is incorrect.

Assumptions – Sample Questions

Now that you've learned what assumptions are, and how to deal with them, it's time to try some sample questions. Find a blank piece of paper and write down your answers to the following questions. Remember that, for each assumption, you should be answering either 'Assumption Made' or 'Assumption Not Made'.

Answers and explanation can be found at the end of this chapter.

> **Note: the contents and statistics used in the questions here are used for testing purposes only. The facts and statistics portrayed in these questions are not necessarily true.**

Question 1

It is vital that we increase public spending on healthcare to keep the population in good health.

Inference 1:	Public spending on healthcare is too low.
Inference 2:	The health of the population is in decline.
Inference 3:	Better healthcare is needed to keep the population healthy.

Question 2

There's no explanation for this increase in sales other than the good publicity the company's been getting. This means that we can raise our budget.

Inference 1:	Good publicity leads to more sales.
Inference 2:	This increase in sales will continue.
Inference 3:	All publicity is good publicity.

Question 3

Pressure groups have begun campaigning for the government to supply more funding for attending afterschool lessons so that nationwide GCSE grades improve. More people should work alongside these pressure groups.

Inference 1:	GCSE grades are currently too low.
Inference 2:	Attending afterschool lessons makes students more likely to perform well at GCSE level.
Inference 3:	Pressure groups can make a difference when it comes to government legislation and strategy.

Question 4

The current government has promised to lower taxes for the working class if they are re-elected. Why should we believe them?

Inference 1:	All governments are corrupt.
Inference 2:	Governments never deliver on their promises.
Inference 3:	The government cannot be trusted.

Question 5

Jeff found the car at the side of the road at 6am. He then drove it to the nearest petrol station and filled the tank with petrol. Then, he drove off, never to be seen again. This is why cars should be fitted with tracking devices.

Inference 1:	The car had a petrol engine and not a diesel engine.
Inference 2:	The car wasn't fitted with a tracking device.
Inference 3:	A tracking device would've stopped Jeff from stealing the car.

Assumptions - Answers

Here are the answers to the assumption sample questions:

Question 1

Assumption 1: Public spending on healthcare is too low.

Answer: Assumption Made.

Explanation: The statement is saying that, in order to keep the population in good health, spending must be increased. Therefore, the statement makes the assumption that the amount spent on healthcare is too low.

Assumption 2: The health of the population is in decline.

Answer: Assumption Not Made.

Explanation: While it's stated that more spending in healthcare is required to keep the population healthy, there's no reason to believe it's *currently* in decline. It might be the case that it will be in decline in the future. The statement is arguing that we should act now. Therefore, this assumption is not being made.

Assumption 3: Better healthcare is needed to keep the population healthy.

Answer: Assumption Made.

Explanation: By increasing the amount of money on healthcare, the quality of care can be higher. This statement is saying that better healthcare is needed in order to keep people healthy. Therefore, it's making the assumption that better healthcare is a necessary part of keeping people healthy.

Question 2

Assumption 1: Good publicity leads to more sales.

Answer: Assumption Made.

Explanation: The statement explicitly claims that the only explanation for the increase in sales is good publicity. Therefore, the statement is relying on the assumption that good publicity leads to more sales.

Assumption 2: This increase in sales will continue.

Answer: Assumption Not Made.

Explanation: While the statement mentions increasing the budget, this doesn't necessarily mean that it's assuming that their sales will continue. They might be able to increase their budget due to the sheer number of sales that they're already had.

Assumption 3: All publicity is good publicity.

Answer: Assumption Not Made.

Explanation: Since the statement explicitly mentions only having good publicity, it seems that it isn't relying on the assumption that all publicity is good publicity.

Question 3

Assumption 1: GCSE grades are currently too low.

Answer: Assumption Made.

Explanation: Since the statement is arguing that we should act to improve GCSE grades, it's making the assumption that GCSE grades are currently too low.

Assumption 2: Attending afterschool lessons makes students more likely to perform well at GCSE level.

Answer: Assumption Made.

Explanation: The statement says that funding afterschool lessons will improve GCSE grades. The assumption being made here is that these afterschool sessions help students improve.

Assumption 3: Pressure groups can make a difference when it comes to government legislation and strategy.

Answer: Assumption Made.

Explanation: The statement argues that more people should work with these pressure groups, implying that it's a worthwhile endeavour. If the person making this claim did not think pressure groups could make a difference, they wouldn't recommend that people contribute to it. Therefore, the statement relies on the assumption that pressure groups can make a difference when it comes to government legislation and strategy.

Question 4

Assumption 1: All governments are corrupt.

Answer: Assumption Not Made.

Explanation: This argument isn't making any sweeping statements about governments as a whole, and therefore it isn't making the assumption that all governments are corrupt. Also, just because a government doesn't fulfil its promises, that doesn't necessarily make it corrupt.

Assumption 2: Governments never deliver on their promises.

Answer: Assumption Not Made.

Explanation: The argument isn't saying that governments never deliver on their promises. What it *is* saying is that governments aren't likely to meet their promises. Therefore, the argument isn't making this assumption.

Assumption 3: The government cannot be trusted.

Answer: Assumption Made.

Explanation: This argument is stating that we don't have much reason to believe that the government will deliver on this promise. Therefore, we cannot trust them or the claims that they are making.

Question 5

Assumption 1: The car had a petrol engine and not a diesel engine.

Answer: Assumption Made.

Explanation: The statement claims that Jeff filled the car up with petrol. Therefore, it makes the assumption that the engine wasn't diesel.

Assumption 2: The car wasn't fitted with a tracking device.

Answer: Assumption Made.

Explanation: The argument made at the end of the passage states that 'more cars should be fitted with tracking devices'. The assumption here is that this car did not have a tracking device.

Assumption 3: A tracking device would've stopped Jeff from stealing the car.

Answer: Assumption Not Made.

Explanation: The statement isn't assuming that the tracking device would have stopped Jeff from stealing the car. Instead, it's assuming that a tracking device would have allowed the police to locate the vehicle.

CRITICAL THINKING
– DEDUCTIONS

In this chapter, we're going to take a look at deductions. The following areas will be discussed:

1. What are deductions?

2. What is a deductive argument?

3. What are deductive validity and deductive soundness?

4. What's the difference between deductive and inductive reasoning?

After that, you'll have the opportunity to answer some sample questions. Explanations for each question are provided at the end of this chapter.

What Are Deductions?

A deduction is a conclusion which is reached logically by examining premises. In fact, a deduction *only* uses its premises in order to reach a conclusion.

Here's a famous example of a logical deduction:

All men are mortal.

Socrates is a man.

Therefore, Socrates is mortal.

Take a look at the following example:

If all cats have tails, and this creature does not have a tail, then it is not a cat.

This is a deductive argument, and can be simplified into the following premises and conclusion:

Premise 1: All cats have tails.

Premise 2: This creature does not have a tail.

Conclusion: This creature is not a cat.

This is a deduction, because it only makes use of the knowledge supplied in the premises in order to reach the conclusion. In other words, each step logically follows on from the next. It begins with the rule that all cats have tails (assumed for the sake of the argument), followed by an acknowledgement that the creature in question does not possess a tail. By using the powers of deduction, we can conclude that this creature is not a cat, because it does not possess a tail.

In the case of this deduction, possessing a tail is a *necessary* condition for being a cat. In order to be a cat, you must possess a tail. However, this does not mean that you are automatically a cat so long as you have a tail. Dogs, horses, and mice also possess tails, but they are not cats. Therefore, possession of a tail is a *necessary* condition for being a cat, but not a *sufficient* one. In other words, all cats have tails, but not all creatures with tails are cats.

Necessary Condition: A statement is definitely false if it doesn't meet this condition. However, meeting this condition doesn't guarantee truth.

Sufficient Condition: A statement is true if it meets this condition. However, this condition isn't necessary for the statement to be true – which implies that there are other conditions which are sufficient.

If a condition is both *necessary* and *sufficient*, then a statement is true if and only if it meets these requirements.

Let's take a look at another example:

Premise 1: This shape has three sides and three corners.

Premise 2: If a shape has three sides and three corners, then it is a triangle.

Conclusion: Therefore, this shape is a triangle.

This is a fairly simply deduction, which involves a condition that is both necessary and sufficient. In order to be a triangle, a shape must have three sides and three corners. In addition, any shape that has three sides and three corners *must* be a triangle.

This deduction follows this structure:

P

If P, then Q

Therefore, Q

This is known as a *syllogism* – a form of deduction reasoning that comes to a conclusion based on two or more propositions, or premises. For any deduction, you can enter the relevant premises and conclusion as replacements for P and Q. For this example, P and Q stand for:

P = 'has three sides and three corners'.

Q = 'is a triangle'.

Then, we need to add our quantifiers. For the sake of this exercise, we're going to use x – which in this case means 'this shape'.

In logical notation, this then becomes:

Px

If Px, then Qx

Therefore, Qx

In formal logic, the quantifier always comes after the proposition – Px, as opposed to xP.

This translates back to:

This shape has three sides and three corners.

If this shape has three sides and three corners, then this shape is a triangle.

Therefore, this shape is a triangle.

This is an example of a deduction in formal logic. You won't need to worry about learning this notation, but it's helpful to get an understanding of how logical deductions work in a more general sense, in order to make sense of them in the Critical Thinking test.

The important thing to take away from this is that, in the test, you'll have three possible deductions. You'll need to work out which are the correct deductions, based on the text. This means that you'll need to look for premises in the text, and find the conclusions which logically follow.

What Are Deduction Questions Like?

Deduction questions in the Critical Thinking test focus on your ability to tell correct deductions from incorrect ones. In other words, you need to figure out which conclusions follow from the premises in the argument.

Here's an example:

Erica owns three small businesses. Anyone who owns three or more small businesses is rich. Therefore:

Conclusion 1: Erica is rich.

Conclusion 2: Erica is not rich.

Conclusion 3: Erica is poor.

Out of these three conclusions, only one follows from the passage. To answer this type of question more easily, you can quickly reformulate it as the following:

Premise 1: Erica owns three small businesses.

Premise 2: Anyone who owns three or more small businesses is rich.

Then, you just need to choose the conclusion which follows from these two premises. In this case, it's conclusion 1.

Premise 1: Erica owns three small businesses.

Premise 2: Anyone who owns three or more small businesses is rich.

Conclusion 1: Erica is rich.

To double-check this, you can reformulate the argument as we did in the previous section:

P = owns three or more small businesses

Q = is rich

Px

If Px, then Qx

Therefore, Qx

This is one way of spotting which conclusion follows from the premises.

For each of these statements, you will need to state whether the conclusion does follow from the premises ('Conclusion Follows') or does not follow ('Conclusion Does Not Follow').

For each passage, you'll get either 3 or 4 possible conclusions to consider.

Deductions – Sample Questions

Now that you've had the chance to learn about deductions in the Critical Thinking test, it's time to apply them to some questions.

For each of these conclusions, you must state whether they follow from the passage ('Conclusion Follows') or don't follow from the passage ('Conclusion Does Not Follow').

Note: the contents and statistics used in the questions here are used for testing purposes only. The facts and statistics portrayed in these questions are not necessarily true.

Question 1

John's company has 220 employees. Companies with less than 250 employees are classified as small businesses. Therefore:

Conclusion 1:   John's company is classified as a big business.
Conclusion 2:   John's company is classified as a small business.
Conclusion 3:   John's company is a small business.

Question 2

Henry is the latest person to receive the most recent training. The person who has received the training most recently is most likely to remember it properly. Therefore:

Conclusion 1:   Henry is most likely to remember the training properly.
Conclusion 2:   Henry is least likely to remember the training properly.
Conclusion 3:   Henry remembers the training better than everyone else.

Question 3

All university graduates who applied were considered for the position. Students who had studied English Literature at degree level were even more likely to get the job. Kerry has a degree, but not in English Literature. Therefore:

Conclusion 1:	Kerry will get the job
Conclusion 2:	Kerry is most likely to get the job.
Conclusion 3:	Kerry could get the job.

Question 4

The library stocks books in specific areas. These are 'Classics', 'Law', '20th Century History' and 'True Crime'. Gemma is currently studying Classics and Psychology, and needs to find a few books on both. Therefore:

Conclusion 1:	Gemma will be able to find the books that she needs here.
Conclusion 2:	Some of the books that Gemma needs will be available in this library, but not all.
Conclusion 3:	Gemma will not find any useful books in this library.

Question 5

All of the second-year students at the university were asked to fill in a questionnaire. A further questionnaire was given to students who planned to take a year abroad for their third year. These students would then have to complete a questionnaire upon returning for their final year. John has filled in 2 questionnaires. Therefore:

Conclusion 1:	John is in his second year, and is not planning to take a year abroad.
Conclusion 2:	John is in his third year after taking a year abroad.
Conclusion 3:	John is in his second year, and plans to take a year abroad.

Deductions – Answers

Question 1

Conclusion 1: John's company is classified as a big business.

Answer: Conclusion Does Not Follow.

Explanation: The passage states that any business with under 250 employees is a small business. John's company has less than 250 employees. Therefore, it cannot be a big business.

Conclusion 2: John's company is classified as a small business.

Answer: Conclusion Follows.

Explanation: The passage states that any business with less than 250 employees is classified as a small business. John's business has less than 250 employees. Therefore, John's company is classified as a small business.

Conclusion 3: John's company is a small business.

Answer: Conclusion Does Not Follow.

Explanation: The passage states that any business with less than 250 employees is *classified* as a small business. It doesn't necessarily follow that John's company *is* a small business, only that it's classified as one.

Question 2

Conclusion 1: Henry is most likely to remember the training properly.

Answer: Conclusion Follows.

Explanation: Since Henry is the most recent person to receive training, and the person who has received the training most recently, he's the most likely to remember the training properly.

Conclusion 2: Henry is least likely to remember the training properly.

Answer: Conclusion Does Not Follow.

Explanation: Henry is the latest person to receive the training. The person who has received the training most recently is most likely to remember it properly. Therefore, Henry is the *most* likely to remember the training properly, not the least likely.

Conclusion 3: Henry remembers the training better than everyone else.

Answer: Conclusion Does Not Follow.

Explanation: The passage only says that Henry is *most* likely to remember the training properly. It does not guarantee that he will remember it better than everyone else, as this conclusion states.

Question 3

Conclusion 1: Kerry will get the job.

Answer: Conclusion Does Not Follow.

Explanation: The people most likely to get the job are those with degrees in English Literature. Kerry does not have a degree in English Literature, therefore she isn't as likely to get the job. This means that there is no guarantee that she'll get the job.

Conclusion 2: Kerry is most likely to get the job.

Answer: Conclusion Does Not Follow.

Explanation: The people most likely to get the job are those with a degree in English Literature. Since Kerry has a degree but not in English Literature, she is not the most likely to get the job.

Conclusion 3: Kerry could get the job.

Answer: Conclusion Follows.

Explanation: Kerry has a university degree. Anyone who has graduated from university will be considered for the position. Therefore, Kerry has a chance of getting the job.

Question 4

Conclusion 1: Gemma will be able to find the books that she needs here.

Answer: Conclusion Does Not Follow.

Explanation: The library doesn't contain any psychology books.

Conclusion 2: Some of the books that Gemma needs will be available in this library, but not all.

Answer: Conclusion Follows.

Explanation: The library contains classics books but not psychology ones. Therefore, only some of the books Gemma needs will be available.

Conclusion 3: Gemma will not find any useful books in this library.

Answer: Conclusion Does Not Follow.

Explanation: Classics books are stocked in the library, and since Gemma takes Classics, at least one of her subjects is covered.

Question 5

Conclusion 1: John is in his second year, and is not planning to take a year abroad.

Answer: Conclusion Does Not Follow.

Explanation: John has taken two questionnaires. A second questionnaire is only given to those who want to study abroad. Therefore, John wants to study abroad.

Conclusion 2: John is in his third year after taking a year abroad.

Answer: Conclusion Does Not Follow.

Explanation: A third questionnaire is given to those who have taken a year abroad. John has only completed two questionnaires. Therefore, John cannot be in third year after taking a year abroad.

Conclusion 3: John is in his second year, and plans to take a year abroad.

Answer: Conclusion Follows.

Explanation: John has taken two questionnaires. A second questionnaire is only given to those who want to study abroad. Therefore, John wants to study abroad and is in his second year.

CRITICAL THINKING
— INTERPRETATIONS

In this chapter, we're going to be discussing interpretations. This will include what they are, as well as how to deal with them.

What Are Interpretations?

An interpretation is a conclusion made from carefully evaluating data, and figuring out what information logically follows from it. We make interpretations every day when going about our lives. For example, if you walk into a supermarket and see a 3 for 2 offer on fruit, you can make the interpretation that this offer will apply to apples, bananas, and pears, whilst also conclude that it will not cover broccoli.

Interpretations are similar to inferences, but focus on whether a conclusion logically follows from a statement, rather than what conclusions are *likely* to follow from a statement. Here, critical thinkers are *interpreting* statements to reveal logically sound information. For example, if it's made clear that there can only be white and black swans in the world, an interpretation of this statement would be that there's no such thing as a green swan.

Questions in this part of the test are usually more complex than this. You're often tasked with showing that you understand the meaning of terms and the significance of data in the passage.

What Are Interpretation Questions Like?

Out of all the questions, interpretation questions are the most likely to include mathematics and scientific data. However, you shouldn't let this worry you if you aren't confident at maths or science. This section is like all of the others in that it's trying to test your critical thinking skills – not your ability to do maths or science.

In the Critical Thinking test, interpretation sections are statements followed by three interpretations. You must decide whether an interpretation follows from the passage ('Conclusion Follows') or does not follow ('Conclusion Does Not Follow'). Rather than point out how likely a claim is to be true, all you need to do here is state whether the interpretation follows from the statement or not.

Take a look at the following example:

The pitch of sounds can be measured by their frequency, such as Hertz (Hz) and Kilohertz (kHz). It is known that human beings can hear sounds in the range of around 20 Hz to 20,000 Hz.

Human speech tends to sit in the range of 1,000 Hz to 5,000 Hz. For comparison, elephants are able to hear sounds in the range of 17 Hz to 10,500 Hz.

Interpretation 1: Humans cannot hear most of the noises made by bats, which occupy the range of 10 kHz to 160 kHz.

Interpretation 2: Humans cannot hear sounds at the frequency of 15 kHz.

Interpretation 3: Elephants can hear a wider range of frequencies than human beings.

Each of these interpretations requires you to read the passage carefully, and see which logically follow from them. Let's take a look at each of them in more detail.

Interpretation 1: Humans cannot hear most of the noises made by bats, which occupy the range of 10 kHz to 160 kHz.

Answer: Conclusion Follows.

Explanation: This interpretation is true because humans can hear up to 20,000 Hz (or 20 kHz). This means that humans can only hear the bat sounds from 10 kHz up to 20 kHz. However, bats make noises up to 160 kHz. This means that most of the noises that bats make cannot be heard by humans.

Interpretation 2: Humans cannot hear sounds at the frequency of 15 kHz.

Answer: Conclusion Does Not Follow.

Explanation: 15 kHz is the same as saying 15,000 Hz. Since we know that humans can hear sounds up to 20,000 Hz (20 kHz), then we can hear sounds at the frequency of 15 kHz.

Interpretation 3: Elephants can hear a wider range of frequencies than human beings.

Answer: Conclusion Does Not Follow.

Explanation: The range that human beings can hear goes from 20 Hz to 20,000 Hz. This is a range of 19,800 Hz. The range that elephants can hear is from 17 Hz to 10,500 Hz. This is a range of 10,483 Hz. Therefore, human beings can hear a wider range of frequencies than elephants.

So, we can see that interpretations are similar to deductions because they both involve examining data available to us, and then coming to conclusions. What you'll likely find is that interpretation questions are more data-heavy than deductions, which mostly deal with simpler 'if, then' statements.

How to Interpret Information From an Argument

The best way to handle an interpretation question in the Critical Thinking test, is to tackle it like a deduction question. After all, your objective in these questions is to highlight which interpretations logically follow from the information provided. The only difference is that you may have to reinterpret phrases.

In the previous example about human and elephant hearing ability, we had to reinterpret Kilohertz (kHz) as Hertz (Hz) in order to make sense of a question. This one is quite straightforward – all you need to do is convert Hz into kHz – but others might be slightly trickier.

For example, a question might mention that candidates who have graduated from university are more likely to get a job, followed by the statement of a candidate who has a degree. In almost all cases, graduating from university involves obtaining a degree. Therefore, it is appropriate to interpret that this means that the candidate who has a degree has also graduated from university. This means that they can be considered for the job.

Interpretations – Sample Questions

Now that you know what interpretations are, it's time to look at some sample questions. Answers will be given at the end of this chapter.

Note: the contents and statistics used in the questions here are used for testing purposes only. The facts and statistics portrayed in these questions are not necessarily true.

Question 1

Everyone works in the office for 8 hours, but they all start at different times. Katie started work at least one hour after everyone else, at 9am. Whomever leaves last must lock up. Therefore:

Interpretation 1:	Everyone else in the office started either before or at 8am.
Interpretation 2:	Katie has to lock up.
Interpretation 3:	Katie started one hour after everyone else.

Question 2

Sarah's business takes in an average of £4,500 per day. Approximately £1,000 goes towards employees, and a further £500 goes towards expenses and maintenance. She then has to pay tax on the rest of her earnings, which is currently set at 45% in Sarah's bracket.

Interpretation 1:	After paying her employees and paying for maintenance, Sarah's business earns £3,000.
Interpretation 2:	Sarah is in the second-highest tax bracket.
Interpretation 3:	Sarah employs ten people.

Question 3

Kenneth cycles for 3 miles every day of the week. Recent health surveys suggest that those who cycle for 20 miles per week are more likely to avoid heart disease. However, studies have also found that cycling for 15 miles or more every week can cause joint damage.

Interpretation 1:	Kenneth is less likely to get heart disease.
Interpretation 2:	Kenneth isn't more likely to get joint damage.
Interpretation 3:	Kenneth cycles for 21 miles per week.

Question 4

A recent study found that students who learn in classes with less than 30 pupils perform better in exams. Jenny's Maths and English classes have 20 pupils in them, while her Physical Education and History classes have 33 pupils in them.

Interpretation 1:	Jenny is more likely to perform better in Maths than in English.
Interpretation 2:	Jenny is more likely to perform better in English than in History.
Interpretation 3:	Jenny is likely to perform better in English than any other subject.

Question 5

Scientists have found a link between faster reflexes and lower sperm counts in males. People who perform well in video games tend to have fast reflexes. People who have fast reflexes also tend to be quite good at tennis. Aaron is very good at video games. Therefore:

Interpretation 1:	Aaron probably has fast reflexes.
Interpretation 2:	Aaron has a low sperm count.
Interpretation 3:	Aaron is probably good at tennis.

Interpretations – Answers

Question 1

Conclusion 1: Everyone else in the office started either before or at 8am.

Answer: Conclusion Follows.

Explanation: The statement says that Katie started work *at least* one hour after everyone else, which happened to be at 9am. This means that, at the latest, everyone else started at 8am.

Conclusion 2: Katie has to lock up.

Answer: Conclusion Follows.

Explanation: Katie was the last to start, and everyone in the office works for the same number of hours. This means that Katie will be the last to leave. According to the passage, the person who leaves last must lock up. Therefore, Katie must lock up.

Conclusion 3: Katie started one hour after everyone else.

Answer: Conclusion Does Not Follow.

Explanation: It's possible that some people started before 8am. This means that Katie would have started over an hour after some people. Therefore, Katie started *at least* one hour after everyone else.

Question 2

Conclusion 1: After paying her employees and paying for maintenance, Sarah's business earns £3,000.

Answer: Conclusion Follows.

Explanation: This involves some simple maths. If Sarah earns £4,500, pays £1,000 to her employees, and pays £500 towards maintenance, then what remains is £3,000.

Conclusion 2: Sarah is in the second-highest tax bracket.

Answer: Conclusion Does Not Follow.

Explanation: This inference does not follow from the original passage, since it doesn't mention what tax bracket Sarah is in.

Conclusion 3: Sarah employs ten people.

Answer: Conclusion Does Not Follow.

Explanation: This inference does not follow from the passage, because there's no information hinting at how many employees Sarah has. All we know is how much Sarah spends on all of them each day. If we knew how much each was paid, it would be possible to figure out how many there were in total with some division. Since this information isn't made available to us, there's no way of figuring this out. Therefore, the inference does not follow.

Question 3

Conclusion 1: Kenneth is less likely to get heart disease.

Answer: Conclusion Follows.

Explanation: Kenneth cycles for 21 miles per week. The surveys suggest that those who cycle for at least 20 miles per week reduce their risk of heart disease. Therefore, Kenneth is less likely to get heart disease.

Conclusion 2: Kenneth isn't more likely to get joint damage.

Answer: Conclusion Does Not Follow.

Explanation: Kenneth cycles for 21 miles per week. Those who cycle for more than 15 miles per week are more likely to get joint damage. Therefore, Kenneth is more likely to get joint damage.

Conclusion 3: Kenneth cycles for 21 miles per week.

Answer: Conclusion Follows.

Explanation: Kenneth cycles for 3 miles every day of the week. There are 7 days in a week. 3 multiplied by 7 equals 21. Therefore, Kenneth cycles for 21 miles per week.

Question 4

Conclusion 1: Jenny is more likely to perform better in Maths than in

English.

Answer: Conclusion Does Not Follow.

Explanation: According to the passage, students in classes with under 30 pupils perform better than students in classes with over 30 pupils. Jenny's Maths and English classes have 20 students in them. Therefore, we can't say for certain that she will perform better in Maths than in English.

Conclusion 2: Jenny is more likely to perform better in English than in History.

Answer: Conclusion Follows.

Explanation: Students in classes with under 30 pupils are likely to perform better than those in classes of over 30 pupils. Jenny's English class has 20 pupils, whilst her History class has 33 pupils. Therefore, she's more likely to perform better in English than History.

Conclusion 3: Jenny is likely to perform better in English than any other subject.

Answer: Conclusion Does Not Follow.

Explanation: Both Jenny's English and Maths classes have less than 30 pupils in them. Therefore, it does not follow that she will perform better in English than *any* of her other subjects.

Question 5

Conclusion 1: Aaron probably has fast reflexes.

Answer: Conclusion Follows.

Explanation: Aaron is good at video games. People who are good at video games tend to have fast reflexes. Therefore, Aaron probably has fast reflexes.

Conclusion 2: Aaron has a low sperm count.

Answer: Conclusion Does Not Follow.

Explanation: People who have fast reflexes *tend* to have a low sperm count. Therefore, there is no *guarantee* that Aaron has a low sperm count, which means that this conclusion does not follow from the premises.

Conclusion 3: Aaron is probably good at tennis.

Answer: Conclusion Does Not Follow.

Explanation: People with fast reflexes tend to be quite good at tennis. Aaron is good at video games, which means he probably has fast reflexes. However, this is too much of a stretch to suggest that because he *probably* has good reflexes, he also *probably* is good at tennis.

CRITICAL THINKING – EVALUATING ARGUMENTS

Along with the aforementioned skills that a critical thinker needs to possess, it's important to be able to evaluate arguments in a more general sense. Critical thinkers need to be able to figure out how strong an argument is by comparing it to the information it's based on.

This can be slightly more abstract than previous areas we've covered. In all of the question types so far, the answers have been relatively straight-forward, with little room for ambiguity or debate. Here, what constitutes a strong or weak argument usually depends on how relevant the argument is, how well-supported it is by the statement, and whether or not it avoids argumentative fallacies.

In this chapter, we'll go through the process of evaluating an argument, including things to look out for which demonstrate that an argument is strong or weak. Then, we'll take a look at how questions about evaluating arguments are formulated in the Critical Thinking test. Then, you'll be able to read and answer some sample questions on evaluating arguments.

What 'Evaluating Arguments' Questions Look Like

In the Critical Thinking test, some of the questions will expect you to evaluate arguments. Like other types of question in the Critical Thinking test, you'll be given a passage first, followed by either three or four arguments about the text. It's your job to go through each of these arguments, and decide on whether they are strong or weak.

This task is straightforward enough on the surface. However, as previously mentioned, there's a lot to consider when answering a question of this kind. Here are some of the things you need to look out for when evaluating an argument:

1. Does the argument commit any informal fallacies, such as the slippery slope, *ad hominem*, gambler's fallacy, argument from popularity, argument from authority, or argument from incredulity?

2. Does the argument follow from the information given in the passage?

3. Does the argument address the topic in the passage and support their argument with evidence?

These are the three major features of an argument that you want to keep an eye out for both during the Critical Thinking test and your daily life. Let's take a look at each of these features in more detail:

Informal Fallacies

We covered informal fallacies in Chapter 4. Most of these could appear in the evaluating arguments questions in the Critical Thinking test. Therefore, you should take some time to read all of the explanations for those arguments, as well as the examples given.

As a general rule, an argument is weak if it relies on an informal fallacy. For example, if an argument only works by making using of a slippery slope, then the argument is weak. Therefore, it's vital that you know what these fallacies are and that you can identify them in an argument.

While some fallacies are well-telegraphed and easy to spot in arguments, this isn't always the case. For example, one argument might include a slippery slope, and even explicitly state that there's the possibility of a slippery slope. For example:

> 'If we make euthanasia legal, this will put us on a slippery slope where eventually people feel that they have the **duty** to die once they get to a certain age, rather than just the **right** to die.'

This is a slippery slope argument made explicit, and therefore is incredibly easy to identify. However, not all fallacies are as easily noticed. For example:

> 'If we make euthanasia legal, then what is currently the **right** to die will become the **duty** to die.'

This is the same argument as the one made above, but without explicit reference to it being a slippery slope. A good way to identify the slippery slope is to see if the argument says that one thing could lead to another, without sufficient evidence to explain why. In particular, this change is suggested to be inevitable, and sets off a chain of events. However, some slippery slopes might cover this up by using the words 'could', or 'might' as opposed to terms which imply inevitability, such as 'will' or 'must'.

In this case, there's no evidence available showing that giving individuals the right to die on their own terms would lead to individuals feeling that they had the duty to die, because they believed themselves to be a burden. Therefore, the argument is stating that one event will lead to another without sufficient evidence.

However, slippery slopes aren't necessarily fallacious. If there is sufficient evidence for one event leading to another, then the slippery slope isn't a fallacious one. However, these cases often aren't referred to as slippery slopes.

One final thing to remember in general about logical fallacies is that, just because an argument contains a fallacy, it doesn't mean that the position that they're defending is incorrect. Rather, it just means that the argument presented, or even just the person who has presented it, is at fault. Someone could defend a completely legitimate position very poorly. For this reason, you shouldn't assume that an entire position is incorrect just because of the way it has been argued. Rather, the argumentation is at fault.

However, for the sake of the Critical Thinking test, it's relatively safe to assume that any argument which contains a logical fallacy is a weak one. Focus on learning your logical fallacies so that you can identify them.

While logical fallacies are the most common causes of a weak argument, there are a couple of other factors which affect how strong an argument is. We'll be taking a look at them next.

A Logical Response

In other sections of the Critical Thinking test, you'll be asked to identify whether a conclusion follows logically from a passage. In both the interpretation and deduction question types, this is asked of you. While this isn't the specific goal of an evaluating arguments question, it is important that you are able to identify when a logical leap has been made.

For example, if the argument creates evidence out of thin air, or it jumps to a conclusion without any steps between to demonstrate this move, then it probably isn't a particularly strong argument.

Evaluating Arguments – Sample Questions

Once you feel comfortable with how to identify strong and weak arguments, take a look at the following sample questions. These should familiarise you with the format of the Critical Thinking test even further. Answers and explanations can be found at the end of the chapter.

For each question, decide whether if the arguments are strong ('Strong Argument') or weak ('Weak Argument').

Note: the contents and statistics used in the questions here are used for testing purposes only. The facts and statistics portrayed in these questions are not necessarily true.

Question 1

Should businesses in London ensure that wages match the living wage for staff living in the city?

Argument 1:	No – staff can live outside of London and commute into the city to work.
Argument 2:	Yes – the alternative would be to force staff to commute, which can lead to increased stress and therefore reduced productivity.
Argument 3:	No – if businesses have to pay more for their staff to live where they want, they could end up having to pay for other luxuries such as private healthcare.

Question 2

Do schools have an obligation to make sure that students study at least one of the Sciences at A-Level?

Argument 1:	Yes – there's a demand for people experienced in the core Sciences in the workplace, so making students take at least one Science subject will increase their job prospects. Since schools should prepare students for the real world, they have an obligation to get them on the right track for a good career.
Argument 2:	No – it isn't the school's responsibility to decide exactly which subjects students choose. Pupils are free to choose the subjects that they want to take, but should be made aware of the possible benefits of studying one of the Sciences at A-Level.
Argument 3:	No – none of the A-Level students that I've met have wanted to do science.

Question 3

The amount of organised crime in major cities has been increasing year on year. The number of armed police officers has also increased year on year. The government is now debating spending money on a new specialised taskforce for organised crime. A number of ex-chiefs of police have commented positively on this. Is this the correct decision?

Argument 1:	No – we can see from the statistics that the increase in number of armed police officers is rising at the same time as the amount of organised crime. A new taskforce would just add to the problem rather than solve it.
Argument 2:	Yes – ex-chiefs of police think that it's a good idea to do it.
Argument 3:	Yes – a specialised taskforce could be completely devoted to the problem of organised crime. In the long-term, this might mean that the government could potentially spend less money on armed police, which has the added benefit of having less police officers with firearms in cities.

Question 4

Out of all the major businesses in London, 90% of them disclose their diversity statistics in an annual report. The rest of the firms are being pressured by investors who believe that a greater focus on diversity would increase annual profit. Should these remaining companies disclose their diversity data?

Argument 1:	Yes – everyone else is doing it, so they should too.
Argument 2:	Yes – the investors think it's a good idea, and if the companies refuse to comply with their suggestions, the investors might pull funds from them.
Argument 3:	No – increasing diversity isn't something that companies should have to do since it's not normal for there to be total equality in terms of ethnicity and gender.

Question 5

Should nurses trained in the UK, and funded by the NHS, be required to work for a certain period of time within the UK public sector before being allowed to work in the private sector or overseas?

Argument 1:	Yes – the NHS funds many of these nurses through training, so they should have to give back for a fixed period of time. This further experience would benefit them as well.
Argument 2:	No – this denies them of their freedom where to work. They might as well be in a work camp.
Argument 3:	Yes – I find it ridiculous that taxpayers' money is spent on training these nurses, only for them to go overseas.

Evaluating Arguments – Answers

Question 1

Argument 1: No – staff can live outside of London and commute into the city to work.

Answer: Weak Argument.

Explanation: This is a weak argument because it fails to acknowledge that commuting also costs money, even though it might be cheaper than living in London. It also fails to acknowledge that commuting costs time.

Argument 2: Yes – the alternative would be to force staff to commute, which can lead to increased stress and therefore reduced productivity.

Answer: Strong Argument.

Explanation: This is a strong argument because it acknowledges that businesses are looking to function as optimally as possible. If they want to achieve this, it's better to avoid forcing staff to commute, since this can decrease productivity. Therefore, businesses have an incentive to ensure that staff can afford to live in the city, preventing long commutes.

Argument 3: No – if businesses have to pay more for their staff to live where they want, they could end up having to pay for other luxuries such as private healthcare.

Answer: Weak Argument.

Explanation: This argument contains a slippery slope fallacy. The belief presented in this argument is that, if businesses match staff wages with the living wage, they will eventually have to pay for other things. This is a slippery slope fallacy because it assumes that one will lead to another, when there's no evidence presented here for it.

Question 2

Argument 1: Yes – there's a demand for people experienced in the core sciences in the workplace, so making students take at least one science subject will increase their job prospects. Since schools should prepare students for the real world, they have an obligation to get them on the right track for a good career.

Answer: Strong Argument.

Explanation: This argument gives a legitimate reason for why schools should force students to take a science at A-Level. One could argue that the purpose of school is to set students up for the real world, and one of the best ways to do this would be to make sure that students have the qualifications to improve their chances of getting a good job.

Argument 2: No – it isn't the school's responsibility to decide exactly which subjects students choose. Pupils are free to choose the subjects that they want to take, but should be made aware of the possible benefits of studying one of the sciences at A-Level.

Answer: Strong Argument.

Explanation: This argument makes the claim that schools don't have the right to dictate exactly what subjects students take. However, it offers a compromise – keeping students informed – which could make sure that more students take a science subject at A-Level.

Argument 3: No – none of the A-Level students that I've met have wanted to do science.

Answer: Weak Argument.

Explanation: This argument relies on anecdotal evidence. The argument is claiming that, because none of the students that they've met are interested in doing science at A-Level, schools should not force students to take them. However, the students that you've met isn't an accurate representation of the entire student population. It might actually be the case that the vast majority of students would want to take sciences. The sample of students cited in this argument isn't enough to establish what the majority of students would want.

Question 3

Argument 1: No – we can see from the statistics that the increase in number of armed police officers is rising at the same time as the amount of organised crime. A new taskforce would just add to the problem rather than solve it.

Answer: Weak Argument.

Explanation: This argument assumes that the correlation between rising crime and number of police officers is a causation. It also assumes that this new taskforce would be just like regular armed police – a conflation of two potentially completely different things.

Argument 2: Yes – ex-chiefs of police think that it's a good idea to do it.

Answer: Weak Argument.

Explanation: This is an appeal to authority, and potentially an appeal to false authority. It doesn't seem that these ex-chiefs of police have given any evidence as to why they believe that this would be a good idea – the argument is simply taking their word for it. Additionally, since they aren't currently chiefs of police, one might question their relevance in the modern era – you could argue that they are a false authority. Either way, this is a weak argument.

Argument 3: Yes – a specialised taskforce could be completely devoted to the problem of organised crime. In the long term, this might mean that the government could potentially spend less money on armed police, which has the added benefit of having less police officers with firearms in cities.

Answer: Strong Argument.

Explanation: This argument recognises that a specialised taskforce is separate to regular armed police, avoiding any conflation.

Question 4

Argument 1: Yes – everyone else is doing it, so they should too.

Answer: Weak Argument.

Explanation: This is an appeal to popularity. The fact that everyone else is doing something, or believes that it is right, does not mean that it is necessarily correct.

Argument 2: Yes – the investors think it's a good idea, and if the companies refuse to comply with their suggestions, the investors might pull funds from them.

Answer: Strong Argument.

Explanation: This argument considers the outcome of not complying with investors. Since a company wants to make money and continue existing, it would be counterproductive to anger their investors.

Argument 3: No – increasing diversity isn't something that companies

should have to do since it's not normal for there to be total equality in terms of ethnicity and gender.

Answer: Weak Argument.

Explanation: This is an appeal to nature, stating that it 'isn't normal' for there to be total inequality. Just because something is considered to be natural or normal, that does not make it correct.

Question 5

Argument 1: Yes – the NHS funds many of these nurses through training, so they should have to give back for a fixed period of time. This further experience would benefit them as well.

Answer: Strong Argument.

Explanation: This argument makes the argument that, since the NHS (and therefore the taxpayer) has funded nurses' training, they owe it to the country's public services to work for them for a period of time. In addition, the argument acknowledges that this experience benefits the nurses as well.

Argument 2: No – this denies them of their freedom where to work. They might as well be in a work camp.

Answer: Weak Argument.

Explanation: This is a false equivalence. Being required to work in the UK is nothing like a forced labour camp, so the speaker is making a comparison that makes these circumstances sound worse than they actually are.

Argument 3: Yes – I find it ridiculous that taxpayers' money is spent on training these nurses, only for them to go overseas.

Answer: Weak Argument.

Explanation: This is an argument from incredulity, as the speaker attaches their own shock of the situation in order to make it seem more unacceptable. In addition, this appears to be an appeal to emotion – by simply mentioning that taxpayers' money is spend on these nurses 'only for them to go overseas', the speaker is trying to make all nurses look guilty in front of an audience – most of whom are presumably taxpayers.

CRITICAL THINKING PRACTICE TEST

Now that you've had the opportunity to familiarise yourself with the content of the Critical Thinking test, the areas you need to learn about, and the type of questions that will be asked, it's time to attempt the Critical Thinking test.

This practice test contains 80 questions. Since the Critical Thinking test usually comes in 40-question or 80-question formats, you can attempt it in one of the following two ways:

a) Take all 80 questions in one sitting, as a single practice test. If you opt for this approach, limit yourself to 60 minutes to complete the whole test.

b) Divide the 80 questions into two sittings – 40 questions for each. If you decide to take the practice test like this, spend 30 minutes on each set of 40 questions.

Bear in mind that the real Critical Thinking test is usually taken at a computer. In the computerised version of the test, you just need to click the answer which you believe is correct.

In this written version of the Critical Thinking test, you can either tick or circle the answer that you think is correct, or you can write your answers down on a spare sheet of paper. Whichever is the case, just remember that the action of answering the questions will be slightly different in the real test. The question format, however, will remain the same.

Finally, remember that there will be either 3 or 4 questions per passage. So, you'll be given one passage for a section, and then you'll be given 3 or 4 arguments, inferences, conclusions, interpretations, or deductions that you'll have to deal with in the exact same way that you've done in the sample questions.

Additionally, there's no guarantee that the questions will be neatly divided into sections. The likelihood is that you'll get questions of different types, one after another. So, once you've finished answering a group of four interpretation questions based on one passage, you might move onto a set of deduction questions. Each question will make the question type clear.

While this might not be the case for the Critical Thinking test that you sit, you might have the opportunity to skip questions if you aren't sure about them, and return to them later. If you find yourself stuck on a question either here in the practice test, or in the real Critical Thinking test, make sure you move onto the next one. On average, you have slightly less than a minute to answer each question. While this is usually plenty of time to answer each question, it can become problematic if you get stuck. Try to be constantly answering questions – if you get stuck on a question, skip it and come back to it at the very end.

If you get to the end of the questions with some time left, make sure you go back and check your answers. The priority is to make sure that every question has been answered, so first make sure that any questions that you might've skipped are answered by the end of the test. If you return to a question and still have no idea what the answer is, it's better to make a guess than leave it blank. However, this shouldn't be relied upon as a method of passing the Critical Thinking test – it should only be used as a last resort.

Note: the contents and statistics used in the questions here are used for testing purposes only. The facts and statistics portrayed in these questions are not necessarily true.

Critical Thinking Practice Test – Part A

Section 1 - Assumptions

Good education is the lifeblood of our country. We need to ensure that class sizes aren't too large by building new schools.

---

1. Young people are a vital part of our country.

Assumption Made/Assumption Not Made

2. People work better in smaller classes.

Assumption Made/Assumption Not Made

3. Class sizes are too large.

Assumption Made/Assumption Not Made

4. Schools are cheap to build.

Assumption Made/Assumption Not Made

Section 2 – Evaluating Arguments

There has been a recent spike in personal data of customers and clients leaking in many UK businesses. Should companies take their clients' data more seriously when it comes to the protection of personal information?

1. Yes – companies have an obligation to make sure that their customers or clients are satisfied. If they have their personal information leaked or stolen, they might not use the service again. This would be bad for the company, because it would lose money.

Strong Argument/Weak Argument

2. No – companies would have to spend money on increasing security, which might not be worth it for them in the long run. This, combined with the fact that another security breach may not happen, means that these companies have no incentive to improve security.

Strong Argument/Weak Argument

3. Yes – it's happened before, and it'll happen again.

Strong Argument/Weak Argument

Section 3 - Inferences

> *A scientific study has found a link between drinking natural spring water and increased performance in the workplace – particularly in office jobs. These researchers are recommending that businesses invest in supplies of bottled spring water to provide to staff if they want to improve productivity.*

1. Scientists believe that there is a causal relationship between drinking spring water and increased productivity.

Definitely True/Probably True/Insufficient data to say whether it is true or false/Probably False/Definitely False

2. Drinking spring water makes you work harder.

Definitely True/Probably True/Insufficient data to say whether it is true or false/Probably False/Definitely False

3. Bottled non-spring water improves productivity.

Definitely True/Probably True/Insufficient data to say whether it is true or false/Probably False/Definitely False

Section 4 - Interpretations

Recent health research conducted in the UK suggests that eating 5 portions of fruit or vegetables per day isn't enough for a healthy lifestyle. The studies show that 10 portions of fruit or vegetables per day is necessary. Currently, it is against the law for packaging on products to be misleading. This means that the '5-a-day' campaign will have to be cancelled and replaced with a '10-a-day' equivalent.

1. Packaging will have to be changed to '10-a-day' rather than '5-a-day'.

Conclusion Follows/Conclusion Does Not Follow

2. The minimum amount of fruit or vegetables necessary to live healthily is 10.

Conclusion Follows/Conclusion Does Not Follow

3. This change from 5 to 10 per day is the result of changes in our environment and the food we eat.

Conclusion Follows/Conclusion Does Not Follow

4. You will live longer if you eat 10 portions of fruit and vegetables per day.

Conclusion Follows/Conclusion Does Not Follow

Section 5 – Assumptions

> *Raising taxes to create a more robust public sector is a good thing because it creates more jobs.*

1. Raising taxes is necessary in order to create more public sector jobs.

Assumption Made/Assumption Not Made

2. More money in the public sector means that more jobs can be made.

Assumption Made/Assumption Not Made

3. The private sector is bad for jobs.

Assumption Made/Assumption Not Made

4. Taxes need to be higher.

Assumption Made/Assumption Not Made

Section 6 - Deductions

> *All secondary school teachers can teach at primary school.*
> *All secondary school teachers trained in England can teach at*
> *secondary schools in England but not in Wales. Therefore:*

1. All secondary school teachers in Wales can teach in England.

Conclusion Follows/Conclusion Does Not Follow

2. All primary school teachers can teach at secondary school.

Conclusion Follows/Conclusion Does Not Follow

3. A secondary school teacher trained in England can teach at a primary or secondary school in England.

Conclusion Follows/Conclusion Does Not Follow

Section 7 – Evaluating Arguments

> *If the government decides to scrap tuition fees for university students, should previous student debts be written off as well?*

1. No – once you start writing off the debt for recent students, you'll have to write off the debt for every student ever.

Strong Argument/Weak Argument

2. Yes – it isn't fair on the students who have just finished university that they continue to pay off a full loan.

Strong Argument/Weak Argument

3. No – instead of wiping their debts off entirely, we can just reduce them. That way, the government still gets some of their money back, whilst ex-students have to pay less debt.

Strong Argument/Weak Argument

Section 8 – Inferences

> *A school report showed that more students than ever were achieving between an A* and a C at A-Level. 2 years ago, the school experienced a surge in GCSE performance, as students were more likely to get an A* than in previous years. In the last year, the school has invested time and resources into afterschool sessions and more vigorous lesson plans.*

1. The students who were achieving high grades at GCSE are now achieving high grades at A-Level.

Definitely True/Probably True/Insufficient data to say whether it is true or false/Probably False/Definitely False

2. Afterschool sessions and better lesson plans have caused the surge in grades at GCSE level.

Definitely True/Probably True/Insufficient data to say whether it is true or false/Probably False/Definitely False

3. Fewer students achieved high grades at GCSE than at A-Level.

Definitely True/Probably True/Insufficient data to say whether it is true or false/Probably False/Definitely False

4. High GCSE grades causes high A-Level grades.

Definitely True/Probably True/Insufficient data to say whether it is true or false/Probably False/Definitely False

Section 9 – Interpretations

Loft insulation saves on heating bills. Leaving the heating on and windows open results in a waste of energy. Wasting energy results in higher energy bills. Alex has loft insulation, but leaves the heating on with the windows open regularly.

1. Alex is saving on heating.

Conclusion Follows/Conclusion Does Not Follow

2. Alex is wasting energy.

Conclusion Follows/Conclusion Does Not Follow

3. Alex is somewhat wasting energy.

Conclusion Follows/Conclusion Does Not Follow

Section 10 – Deductions

All doctors must study medicine at university. This takes five years at university, and beyond that training can take up to sixteen years in total to fully qualify. Nicola is 8 years into her training as a doctor. Therefore:

1. Nicola has finished studying medicine at university.

Conclusion Follows/Conclusion Does Not Follow

2. Nicola is now a fully-qualified doctor.

Conclusion Follows/Conclusion Does Not Follow

3. Nicola is still training to be a doctor.

Conclusion Follows/Conclusion Does Not Follow

Section 11 – Inferences

> *Tourism research suggests that the Royal Family generates approximately £500 million in tourism per year. Tourism in general generates approximately £3 billion per year. On the years where there is a special occasion such as a jubilee or royal wedding, this number can increase by a further 60%. In particular, locations such as Buckingham Palace and Westminster Abbey see the most tourists.*

1. People come to the UK to visit Buckingham Palace.

Definitely True/Probably True/Insufficient data to say whether it is true or false/Probably False/Definitely False

2. The Royal Family contributes to approximately 16% of the total money generated by tourists.

Definitely True/Probably True/Insufficient data to say whether it is true or false/Probably False/Definitely False

3. More tourists come to the UK during special years which include jubilees or royal weddings.

Definitely True/Probably True/Insufficient data to say whether it is true or false/Probably False/Definitely False

Section 12 – Deductions

Everyone in the UK who carries a firearm is either a criminal, a farmer, or a police officer. If they are carrying an illegal weapon, then they are a criminal. If they have a shotgun and a license, they are a farmer, and if they're in the police force, they're a police officer. Hannah possesses an illegal weapon, as well as a shotgun license and a shotgun. Eric is in the police force. Therefore:

1. Eric possesses a firearm.

Conclusion Follows/Conclusion Does Not Follow

2. Hannah is a criminal.

Conclusion Follows/Conclusion Does Not Follow

3. Hannah is a criminal as well as a farmer.

Conclusion Follows/Conclusion Does Not Follow

Critical Thinking Practice Test – Part B

Section 1 – Evaluating Arguments

> *In cases where individuals are terminally ill and suffering, should euthanasia (assisted suicide) be legalised?*

1. No – it isn't natural for people to end their lives in such a way.

Strong Argument/Weak Argument

2. Yes – individuals have the right to decide what happens to their own bodies. If a terminally-ill person is incapable of taking his or her own life, medical support should be accessible to allow them to die on their own terms.

Strong Argument/Weak Argument

3. No – instead of funding support and services to help people die, that money should instead be spent on researching these terminal illnesses in order to find cures and better palliative treatment.

Strong Argument/Weak Argument

Section 2 – Interpretations

In 2007, the number of people buying MP3 players skyrocketed, which in turn popularised the MP3 file format. In 2017, the MP3 is significantly less popular, which some assume is due to the rise in popularity of streaming services. Streaming services do not require this type of file. In 2008, Ryan developed a piece of software which allowed people who bought it to convert audio files to MP3. Now, he's going to have to cease development of it.

1. Ryan had to cease development of the software, because MP3 has declined in popularity.

Conclusion Follows/Conclusion Does Not Follow

2. MP3 is in decline because less people use MP3 files.

Conclusion Follows/Conclusion Does Not Follow

3. The rise of MP3 players inevitably led to the eventual downfall of the MP3 file format.

Conclusion Follows/Conclusion Does Not Follow

Section 3 – Assumptions

> *Technology companies who specialise in handheld devices such as tablets and smartphones should invest in making their products more intuitive for elderly people. This demographic hasn't been tapped into yet and could greatly benefit from such devices.*

1. Elderly people would like to buy tablets and smartphones.

Assumption Made/Assumption Not Made

2. Elderly people struggle with new technology.

Assumption Made/Assumption Not Made

3. Technology companies aren't already investing in this area.

Assumption Made/Assumption Not Made

4. Apps which are more suitable for elderly people are in development.

Assumption Made/Assumption Not Made

Section 4 – Inferences

A modern 'reboot' of an old Science Fiction film has released to critical and commercial acclaim. It contained some of the features of the original, but critics were most impressed by the risks it took, and how willing it was to differ from the movie it was based on. Surveys and review aggregate websites found that audiences were also pleased with the movie.

1. This film did well commercially because it differed from the original.

Definitely True/Probably True/Insufficient data to say whether it is true or false/Probably False/Definitely False

2. Audiences love science fiction movies.

Definitely True/Probably True/Insufficient data to say whether it is true or false/Probably False/Definitely False

3. This film reviewed well because it differed from the original.

Definitely True/Probably True/Insufficient data to say whether it is true or false/Probably False/Definitely False

Section 5 – Assumptions

In 2014, the Prime Minister guaranteed that the 'triple-lock' set in place to protect pensions would not be removed. In 2017, the government suggested that they would have to remove the triple-lock to maintain economic stability. While this may cause issues for pensioners, it is beneficial overall for the economy. However, the government should be held responsible for breaking their own promise.

1. The government proposing to remove the triple-lock is the same one which promised to protect it.

Assumption Made/Assumption Not Made

2. The economy is currently strong.

Assumption Made/Assumption Not Made

3. The government should protect pensioners' interests.

Assumption Made/Assumption Not Made

Section 6 – Evaluating Arguments

Should the government invest more money on developing its nuclear arsenal?

1. Yes – tensions are rising between the nations with nuclear weapons, and therefore we must maintain a strong nuclear deterrent.

Strong Argument/Weak Argument

2. Yes – everyone else is doing it, so we should as well.

Strong Argument/Weak Argument

3. Yes – if we cut our nuclear arsenal, what's next? We might also end up downscaling our navy or air force.

Strong Argument/Weak Argument

4. No – by refusing to take part in a nuclear arms race, we would be sending a message that we aren't afraid, and others would follow.

Strong Argument/Weak Argument

Section 7 – Deductions

> *Before 2015, Katie employed staff who did not have a driving license. In 2015, Katie made it a requirement for applicants to have a driving license **and** a car in order to apply for a job. Before 2015, applicants required 3 A-Levels to get a job at Katie's company. In 2015, Katie reduced that to two. Angela works for Katie, has three A-Levels but no driving license. Jim is going to apply for a job at Katie's business – he has 2 A-Levels and no driving license. Liam has 2 A-Levels and a driving license, and works for Katie.*

1. Jim could have got a job before 2015, but cannot now.

Conclusion Follows/Conclusion Does Not Follow

2. Angela started working for Katie before 2015.

Conclusion Follows/Conclusion Does Not Follow

3. Jim has a car.

Conclusion Follows/Conclusion Does Not Follow

4. Liam started working for Katie in 2015 or later.

Conclusion Follows/Conclusion Does Not Follow

Section 8 – Assumptions

> *The government has decided to pardon homosexual people who had been convicted of homosexuality in the past. This is a positive but long overdue response to historical injustice.*

1. The government should make amends for the mistakes that previous ones made.

Assumption Made/Assumption Not Made

2. The fact that these individuals were convicted in the first place is a historical injustice.

Assumption Made/Assumption Not Made

3. Previous governments weren't homophobic.

Assumption Made/Assumption Not Made

4. This should have happened sooner.

Assumption Made/Assumption Not Made

Section 9 – Inferences

> *Anti-Social Behaviour Orders were introduced in 1998 to help reduce anti-social behaviour among young people in the UK. In 2004, studies found that the number of incidents of anti-social behaviour being reported had increased to 100,000, while it was only 60,000 per year before 1998.*

1. Anti-Social Behaviour Orders have caused more anti-social behaviour in the UK.

Definitely True/Probably True/Insufficient data to say whether it is true or false/Probably False/Definitely False

2. People are more willing to report anti-social behaviour because the Anti-Social Behaviour Order exists.

Definitely True/Probably True/Insufficient data to say whether it is true or false/Probably False/Definitely False

3. The amount of anti-social behaviour in the UK has increased since 1998.

Definitely True/Probably True/Insufficient data to say whether it is true or false/Probably False/Definitely False

4. The amount of anti-social behaviour has increased every year since 1998.

Definitely True/Probably True/Insufficient data to say whether it is true or false/Probably False/Definitely False

Section 10 – Deductions

Not everyone who owns a car has a driving license, and not everyone who owns a driving license owns a car. Everyone who has a driving license has taken their driving test. However, everyone who drives on the road has a driving license, but might not own a car. Jack drives on the road. Therefore:

1. Jack owns a car.

Conclusion Follows/Conclusion Does Not Follow

2. Jack has a driving license.

Conclusion Follows/Conclusion Does Not Follow

3. Jack has taken his driving test.

Conclusion Follows/Conclusion Does Not Follow

4. All drivers on the road have taken their driving test.

Conclusion Follows/Conclusion Does Not Follow

Section 11 – Evaluating Arguments

Should it be illegal for individuals working at a company to become whistle-blowers, leaking information to expose perceived injustice?

1. No – companies should be held accountable for breaking the law or being immoral, and the general public has a right to know about this because the behaviour of these companies affects society.

Strong Argument/Weak Argument

2. Yes – employees leaking information about their employer is no different to a soldier leaking military secrets.

Strong Argument/Weak Argument

3. Yes – whistle-blowers should be punished but should only receive a suspended sentence or a fine.

Strong Argument/Weak Argument

Section 12 – Inferences

In 2016, a record number of university students appeared at a protest in London against the current government. Recently, the government suggested that they would be raising tuition fees from £9,000 to a higher value. Student unions across the country stated that they would be advocating and organising protests at Westminster if the government suggested raising tuition fees to over £10,000 per year. These unions mobilised for protests in 2016.

1. The government planned to raise tuition fees to over £10,000 per year.

Definitely True/Probably True/Insufficient data to say whether it is true or false/Probably False/Definitely False

2. Students were protesting because of the proposed rise in tuition fees.

Definitely True/Probably True/Insufficient data to say whether it is true or false/Probably False/Definitely False

3. It is only students that are protesting at Westminster.

Definitely True/Probably True/Insufficient data to say whether it is true or false/Probably False/Definitely False

CRITICAL THINKING PRACTICE TEST – ANSWERS

Now that you've had a chance to complete the practice test, take some time to read through the answers in this chapter. Make sure that you read the explanations for both answers that you got right and those you got wrong. This is so you know that you arrived at the correct answers for the right reasons. You'll also be able to work out where you went wrong for the answers that you got wrong.

Critical Thinking Practice Test – Part A

Section 1 – Assumptions

> *Good education is the lifeblood of our country. We need to ensure that class sizes aren't too large by building new schools.*

1.

Statement: Young people are a vital part of our country.

Answer: Assumption Made.

Explanation: The passage states that good education is the 'lifeblood' of our country, stating that it is vital. Since education mostly affects young people, it is fair to say that the passage assumes that young people are a vital part of our country.

2.

Statement: People work better in smaller classes.

Answer: Assumption Made.

Explanation: The argument says that 'good education' is vital for the country. It then states that class sizes need to stay smaller. The assumption here is that smaller classes will make sure that education is good.

3.

Statement: Class sizes are too large.

Answer: Assumption Not Made.

Explanation: The passage states that we need to build new schools to ensure that class sizes aren't too large. However, it does not state that classes are currently too large; it could be referring to a future need for more schools to ensure class overcrowding does not become a problem as the population grows.

4.

Statement: Schools are cheap to build.

Answer: Assumption Not Made.

Explanation: There's no mention of how expensive schools are in the passage. Therefore, this passage does not make the assumption that schools are cheap to build.

Section 2 – Evaluating Arguments

> *There has been a recent spike in personal data of customers and clients leaking in many UK businesses. Should companies take their clients' data more seriously when it comes to the protection of personal information?*

1.

Statement: Yes – companies have an obligation to make sure that their customers or clients are satisfied. If they have their personal information leaked or stolen, they might not use the service again. This would be bad for the company because it would lose money.

Answer: Strong Argument.

Explanation: This is a strong argument because it considers the possible outcomes of making this decision, as well as what the goals of the company are.

2.

Statement: No – companies would have to spend money on increasing security, which might not be worth it for them in the long run. This, combined with the fact that another security breach may not happen, means that these companies have no incentive to improve security.

Answer: Strong Argument.

Explanation: This argument assesses the likelihood of another cyber-attack, and makes the reasonable claim that another might not happen. Therefore, it isn't worth the expense.

3.

Statement: Yes – it's happened before, and it'll happen again.

Answer: Weak Argument.

Explanation: This argument is an induction based on little evidence. Just because something happened once, that does not necessarily mean it will happen again.

Section 3 – Inferences

> *A scientific study has found a link between drinking natural spring water and increased performance in the workplace – particularly in office jobs. These researchers are recommending that businesses invest in supplies of bottled spring water to provide to staff if they want to improve productivity.*

1.

Statement: Scientists believe that there is a causal relationship between drinking spring water and increased productivity.

Answer: Probably True.

Explanation: It is probably the case that scientists believe this, since they are now recommending that businesses invest in supplies of bottled spring water. This is not 'definitely true' because it's possible that the scientists could have a vested interest of some kind in recommending the bottled water.

2.

Statement: Drinking spring water makes you work harder.

Answer: Insufficient data to say whether it is true or false.

Explanation: We cannot assume that bottled spring water makes you work harder. It could simply be a correlation, and this does not imply causation.

3.

Statement: Bottled non-spring water improves productivity.

Answer: Insufficient data to say whether it is true or false.

Explanation: The text makes no mention of bottled non-spring water. Therefore, there isn't evidence to state whether this is true or false.

Section 4 – Interpretations

> *Recent health research conducted in the UK suggests that eating 5 portions of fruit or vegetables per day isn't enough for a healthy lifestyle. The studies show that 10 portions of fruit or vegetables per day is necessary. Currently, it is against the law for packaging on products to be misleading. This means that the '5-a-day' campaign will have to be cancelled and replaced with a '10-a-day' equivalent.*

1.

Statement: Packaging will have to be changed to '10-a-day' rather than '5-a-day'.

Answer: Conclusion Follows.

Explanation: Since it's against the law for packaging to be misleading, and because '5-a-day' is no longer accurate, it will have to be changed to '10-a-day'.

2.

Statement: The minimum amount of fruit or vegetables necessary to live healthily is 10.

Answer: Conclusion Follows.

Explanation: From the information in the passage, we can interpret that 10 fruit or vegetables per day is necessary for a healthy lifestyle.

3.

Statement: This change from 5 to 10 per day is the result of changes in our environment and the food we eat.

Answer: Conclusion Does Not Follow.

Explanation: This isn't necessarily true – it might just be the case that researchers were wrong before, and there hasn't been a physiological or environmental change.

4.

Statement: You will live longer if you eat 10 portions of fruit and vegetables per day.

Answer: Conclusion Does Not Follow.

Explanation: There's no guarantee that eating 10 portions of fruit and vegetables per day will make you live longer.

Section 5 – Assumptions

> *Raising taxes to create a more robust public sector is a good thing because it creates more jobs.*

1.

Statement: Raising taxes is necessary in order to create more public-sector jobs.

Answer: Assumption Made.

Explanation: The text states that raising taxes boosts the public sector. It then states that this will create more jobs.

2.

Statement: More money in the public sector means that more jobs can be made.

Answer: Assumption Made.

Explanation: The passage states that, by raising taxes, there will be more money in the public sector. It also states that a more robust public sector creates more jobs. Therefore, it assumes that more money in the public sector means that more jobs can be made.

3.

Statement: The private sector is bad for jobs.

Answer: Assumption Not Made.

Explanation: The text makes no reference to the private sector. Just because it prefers the public sector, that does not mean there is the assumption that the private sector is bad for jobs.

4.

Statement: Taxes need to be higher.

Answer: Assumption Made.

Explanation: The passage is stating that raising taxes would be beneficial. Therefore, the assumption is that taxes need to be higher.

Section 6 – Deductions

> *All secondary school teachers can teach at primary school.*
> *All secondary school teachers trained in England can teach at secondary schools in England but not in Wales. Therefore:*

1.

Statement: All secondary school teachers in Wales can teach in England.

Answer: Conclusion Does Not Follow.

Explanation: From the text, there's no way to tell whether a secondary school teacher trained in Wales can also teach in England.

2.

Statement: All primary school teachers can teach at secondary school.

Answer: Conclusion Does Not Follow.

Explanation: According to the passage, all secondary school teachers can teach at primary school. However, there is no confirmation that all primary school teachers can teach at secondary school. Therefore, the conclusion does not follow.

3.

Statement: A secondary school teacher trained in England can teach at a primary or secondary school in England.

Answer: Conclusion Follows.

Explanation: The passage states that 'all secondary school teachers can teach at primary school.' Therefore, a secondary school teacher trained in England can teach at a primary or secondary school in England.

Section 7 – Evaluating Arguments

If the government decides to scrap tuition fees for university students, should previous student debts be written off as well?

1.

Statement: No – once you start writing off the debt for recent students, you'll have to write off the debt for every student ever.

Answer: Weak Argument.

Explanation: This is an example of a slippery slope fallacy. There could quite easily be a 'cut-off' point along the timeline of students finishing. Therefore, you wouldn't need to write off the debt for every student.

2.

Statement: Yes – it isn't fair on the students who have just finished university that they continue to pay off a full loan.

Answer: Weak Argument.

Explanation: This is an appeal to emotion, and doesn't give a legitimate reason to pay off student debts.

3.

Statement: No – instead of wiping their debts off entirely, we can just reduce them. That way, the government still gets some of their money back, whilst ex-students have to pay less debt.

Answer: Weak Argument.

Explanation: This is an argument to moderation, as it makes a compromise between two parties, and fails to properly satisfy either.

Section 8 – Inferences

A school report showed that more students than ever were achieving between an A* and a C at A-Level. 2 years ago, the school experienced a surge in GCSE performance, as students were more likely to get an A* than in previous years. In the last year, the school has invested time and resources into afterschool sessions and more vigorous lesson plans.

1.

Statement: The students who were achieving high grades at GCSE are now achieving high grades at A-Level.

Answer: Probably True.

Explanation: There's a 2-year gap between GCSE and A-Level exams. It's reasonable to assume that at least some of the students who achieved high scores at GCSE also did well at A-Level.

2.

Statement: Afterschool sessions and better lesson plans have caused the surge in grades at GCSE level.

Answer: Definitely False.

Explanation: The school invested resources into afterschool sessions and better lesson plans in the past year. However, the surge in GCSE grades occurred 2 years ago.

3.

Statement: Fewer students achieved high grades at GCSE than at A-Level.

Answer: Insufficient data to say whether it is true or false.

Explanation: The passage doesn't mention which level got more high grades in it.

4.

Statement: High GCSE grades causes high A-Level grades.

Answer: Insufficient data to say whether it is true or false.

Explanation: We can't assume a causal relationship between high GCSE grades and high A-level grades. We can only acknowledge a correlation.

Section 9 – Interpretations

> *Loft insulation saves on heating bills. Leaving the heating on and windows open results in a waste of energy. Wasting energy results in higher energy bills. Alex has loft insulation, but leaves the heating on with the windows open regularly.*

1.

Statement: Alex is saving on heating.

Answer: Conclusion Does Not Follow.

Explanation: Alex has loft insulation, which saves on heating, but also leaves the heating on, which wastes energy. Since wasting energy results in higher energy bills, this means that Alex is not saving on heating.

2.

Statement: Alex is wasting energy.

Answer: Conclusion Follows.

Explanation: Alex leaves the heating on and the windows open, which are two of the things which waste energy. Therefore, Alex is wasting energy.

3.

Statement: Alex is somewhat wasting energy.

Answer: Conclusion Follows.

Explanation: We know from the text that Alex is wasting energy. Therefore, Alex must also be somewhat wasting energy.

Section 10 – Deductions

> *All doctors must study medicine at university. This takes five years at university, and beyond that training can take up to sixteen years in total to fully qualify. Nicola is 8 years into her training as a doctor. Therefore:*

1.

Statement: Nicola has finished studying medicine at university.

Answer: Conclusion Follows.

Explanation: Nicola is 8 years into her training. University takes five years. Therefore, Nicola has finished studying medicine at university.

2.

Statement: Nicola is now a fully-qualified doctor.

Answer: Conclusion Does Not Follow.

Explanation: The passage states that Nicola is 8 years into her training. Training can take up to 16 years. Therefore, we cannot conclude that she is now a fully-qualified doctor.

3.

Statement: Nicola is still training to be a doctor.

Answer: Conclusion Follows.

Explanation: The passage says that Nicola is 8 years into her training, rather than saying that she is now qualified. Therefore, we can conclude that Nicola is still training to be a doctor.

Section 11 – Inferences

> *Tourism research suggests that the Royal Family generates approximately £500 million in tourism per year. Tourism in general generates approximately £3 billion per year. On the years where there is a special occasion such as a jubilee or royal wedding, this number can increase by a further 60%. In particular, locations such as Buckingham Palace and Westminster Abbey see the most tourists.*

1.

Statement: People come to the UK to visit Buckingham Palace.

Answer: Definitely True.

Explanation: The passage says that location such as Buckingham palaces see the most tourists. Therefore, we can conclude that at least some people come to the UK to visit Buckingham Palace.

2.

Statement: The Royal Family contributes to approximately 16% of the total money generated by tourism.

Answer: Definitely True.

Explanation: £500 million is approximately 16% of £3 billion. Therefore, the Royal Family generates approximately 16% of the total money generated by tourism.

3.

Statement: More tourists come to the UK during special years, which include jubilees or royal weddings.

Answer: Probably True.

Explanation: More money from tourism does not necessarily mean that there are more tourists – people could just be spending more – but it's *likely* that there are more tourists visiting during this time.

Section 12 – Deductions

Everyone in the UK who carries a firearm is either a criminal, a farmer, or a police officer. If they are carrying an illegal weapon, then they are a criminal. If they have a shotgun and a license, they are a farmer, and if they're in the police force, they're a police officer. Hannah possesses an illegal weapon, as well as a shotgun license and a shotgun. Eric is in the police force. Therefore:

1.

Statement: Eric possesses a firearm.

Answer: Conclusion Does Not Follow.

Explanation: Just because Eric is in the police, this does not mean he possesses a firearm.

2.

Statement: Hannah is a criminal.

Answer: Conclusion Follows.

Explanation: Everyone who owns an illegal firearm is a criminal. Hannah owns an illegal firearm. Therefore, Hannah is a criminal.

3.

Statement: Hannah is a criminal as well as a farmer.

Answer: Conclusion Follows.

Explanation: Everyone who owns an illegal firearm is a criminal. Hannah owns an illegal firearm. Therefore, Hannah is a criminal. In addition, everyone who owns a shotgun and shotgun license is a farmer. Hannah owns a shotgun and shotgun license. Therefore, Hannah is also a farmer.

Critical Thinking Practice Test – Part B

Section 1 – Evaluating Arguments

> *In cases where individuals are terminally ill and suffering, should euthanasia (assisted suicide) be legalised?*

1.

Statement: No – it isn't natural for people to end their lives in such a way.

Answer: Weak Argument.

Explanation: This is an appeal to nature. Just because something is unnatural, as is suggested about euthanasia, this does not make it immoral.

2.

Statement: Yes – individuals have the right to decide what happens to their own bodies. If a terminally-ill person is incapable of taking his or her own life, medical support should be accessible to allow them to die on their own terms.

Answer: Strong Argument.

Explanation: This argument considers the rights that a human being has to control their own body, and makes the judgement that if an individual cannot take their own life due to physical inability, they should be allowed assistance.

3.

Statement: No – instead of funding support and services to help people die, that money should instead be spent on researching these terminal illnesses in order to find cures and better palliative treatment.

Answer: Weak Argument.

Explanation: This is a false dichotomy, as it suggests that we can either fund euthanasia *or* cures and palliative treatment. There's no reason to believe that we can only choose one or the other.

Section 2 – Interpretations

> *In 2007, the number of people buying MP3 players skyrocketed, which in turn popularised the MP3 file format. In 2017, the MP3 is significantly less popular, which some assume is due to the rise in popularity of streaming services. Streaming services do not require this type of file. In 2008, Ryan developed a piece of software which allowed people who bought it to convert audio files to MP3. Now, he's going to have to cease development of it.*

1.

Statement: Ryan has to cease development of the software because MP3 has declined in popularity.

Answer: Conclusion Does Not Follow.

Explanation: While it's likely that Ryan has to cease development due to a decline in popularity, this isn't made explicit. There may be other explanations which are not referenced in the text.

2.

Statement: MP3 is in decline because less people use MP3 files.

Answer: Conclusion Follows.

Explanation: The popularity of MP3 depends on how many people use it. Therefore, MP3 must be in decline because less people are using MP3 files.

3.

Statement: The rise of MP3 players inevitably led to the eventual downfall of the MP3 file format.

Answer: Conclusion Does Not Follow.

Explanation: There's no reason to believe that the rise of MP3 players caused the downfall of the MP3 file format.

Section 3 – Assumptions

> *Technology companies who specialise in handheld devices such as tablets and smartphones should invest in making their products more intuitive for elderly people. This demographic hasn't been tapped into yet and could greatly benefit from such devices.*

1.

Statement: Elderly people would like to buy tablets and smartphones.

Answer: Assumption Made.

Explanation: The passage states that companies should invest in making these devices more suitable for the elderly. However, they should only invest in this if they can make money for it. This means that there must be a market for devices, which in turn assumes that elderly people want to purchase these devices.

2.

Statement: Elderly people struggle with new technology.

Answer: Assumption Made.

Explanation: The passage states that technology companies' products can be made more intuitive for elderly people. The assumption made by the passage is that elderly people struggle with technology.

3.

Statement: Technology companies aren't already investing in this area.

Answer: Assumption Made.

Explanation: The passage states that the elderly demographic hasn't already been tapped into yet, which suggests that technology companies aren't considering this area. In turn, this suggests that the passage is assuming that technology companies aren't investing in this field, either.

4.

Statement: Apps which are more suitable for elderly people are in development.

Answer: Assumption Not Made.

Explanation: The passage does not allude to apps at any point. Therefore, it does not assume that apps for elderly people are in development.

Section 4 – Inferences

> *A modern 'reboot' of an old Science Fiction film has released to critical and commercial acclaim. It contained some of the features of the original, but critics were most impressed by the risks it took, and how willing it was to differ from the movie it was based on. Surveys and review aggregate websites found that audiences were also pleased with the movie.*

1.

Statement: This film did well commercially because it differed from the original.

Answer: Insufficient data to say whether it is true or false.

Explanation: While the film reviewed well because it differed from the original, that does not mean it performed well commercially for the same reasons. Audiences might not have enjoyed it for the same reasons that critics enjoyed it for.

2.

Statement: Audiences love science fiction movies.

Answer: Insufficient data to say whether it is true or false.

Explanation: While audiences liked this science fiction film in particular, there's no way of telling from this passage that audiences enjoy science fiction movies in general.

3.

Statement: This film reviewed well because it differed from the original.

Answer: Definitely True.

Explanation: The passage states that critics were impressed by the film's willingness to differ from the original, and it reviewed well. Therefore, there is a direct connection between this and reviews.

Section 5 – Assumptions

> *In 2014, the Prime Minister guaranteed that the 'triple-lock' set in place to protect pensions would not be removed. In 2017, the government suggested that they would have to remove the triple-lock to maintain economic stability. While this may cause issues for pensioners, it is beneficial overall for the economy. However, the government should be held responsible for breaking their own promise.*

1.

Statement: The government proposing to remove the triple-lock is the same one which promised to protect it.

Answer: Assumption Made.

Explanation: The passage states that the government should be held responsible for breaking their own promise. This assumes that the same government is in place now that made the promise in 2014.

2.

Statement: The economy is currently strong.

Answer: Assumption Made.

Explanation: The passage states that the removal of the triple-lock is to *maintain* a strong economy. This suggests that the economy is currently strong.

3.

Statement: The government should protect pensioners' interests.

Answer: Assumption Made.

Explanation: The passage says that the government should be held responsible. This assumes that the government has an obligation to protect pensioners' interests.

Section 6 – Evaluating Arguments

Should the government invest more money on developing its nuclear arsenal?

1.

Statement: Yes – tensions are rising between the nations with nuclear weapons, and therefore we must maintain a strong nuclear deterrent.

Answer: Strong Argument.

Explanation: This argument carefully considers the current state of affairs without falling into fallacy. Therefore, it is a strong argument.

2.

Statement: Yes – everyone else is doing it, so we should as well.

Answer: Weak Argument.

Explanation: This is a bandwagon argument. Just because everyone else is doing something, this does not mean that they are right in doing so.

3.

Statement: Yes – if we cut our nuclear arsenal, what's next? We might also end up downscaling our navy or air force.

Answer: Weak Argument.

Explanation: This is a slippery slope. Cutting the nuclear arsenal does not necessarily mean that other parts of the armed forces will be downscaled.

4.

Statement: No – by refusing to take part in a nuclear arms race, we would be sending a message that we aren't afraid, and others would follow.

Answer: Weak Argument.

Explanation: This argument assumes that 'sending a message' would definitely work. There's no reason to believe this. Therefore, this is a weak argument.

Section 7 – Deductions

> *Before 2015, Katie employed staff who did not have a driving license. In 2015, Katie made it a requirement for applicants to have a driving license **and** a car in order to apply for a job. Before 2015, applicants required 3 A-Levels to get a job at Katie's company. In 2015, Katie reduced that to two. Angela works for Katie, has three A-Levels but no driving license. Jim is going to apply for a job at Katie's business – he has 2 A-Levels and no driving license. Liam has 2 A-Levels and a driving license, and works for Katie.*

1.

Statement: Jim could have got a job before 2015, but cannot now.

Answer: Conclusion Does Not Follow.

Explanation: Jim has 2 A-Levels and no driving license. To have got a job before 2015, he would have needed 3 A-Levels. Therefore, Jim could not have got a job before 2015.

2.

Statement: Angela started working for Katie before 2015.

Answer: Conclusion Follows.

Explanation: Angela has 3 A-Levels, no driving license, and works for Katie. To have started working for her after 2015, she would need a driving license. Therefore, she started working for Katie before 2015.

3.

Statement: Jim has a car.

Answer: Conclusion Does Not Follow.

Explanation: There is nothing to suggest that Jim does or does not have a car, therefore the conclusion does not follow.

4.

Statement: Liam started working for Katie in 2015 or later.

Answer: Conclusion Follows.

Explanation: Liam only has 2 A-Levels, which would not have been enough before 2014. Since he has 2 A-Levels and works for Katie, he must have started working for her in 2015 or later.

Section 8 – Assumptions

> *The government has decided to pardon homosexual people who had been convicted of homosexuality in the past. This is a positive but long overdue response to historical injustice.*

1.

Statement: The government should make amends for the mistakes that previous ones made.

Answer: Assumption Made.

Explanation: The passage says that this is 'long overdue', which assumes that the government is responsible for making amends for the acts of previous governments.

2.

Statement: The fact that these individuals were convicted in the first place is a historical injustice.

Answer: Assumption Made.

Explanation: The passage calls these convictions a 'historical injustice'. Therefore, this passage assumes that this is a historical injustice.

3.

Statement: Previous governments weren't homophobic.

Answer: Assumption Not Made.

Explanation: The passage assumes that previous governments *were* homophobic because they enforced homophobic laws.

4.

Statement: This should have happened sooner.

Answer: Assumption Made.

Explanation: The passage says that this is 'long overdue'. The assumption here is that this should have happened sooner.

Section 9 – Inferences

> *Anti-Social Behaviour Orders were introduced in 1998 to help reduce anti-social behaviour among young people in the UK. In 2004, studies found that the number of incidents of anti-social behaviour being reported had increased to 100,000, while it was only 60,000 per year before 1998.*

1.

Statement: Anti-Social Behaviour Orders have caused more anti-social behaviour in the UK.

Answer: Insufficient data to say whether it is true or false.

Explanation: There's a correlation between anti-social behaviour being reported and the introduction of Anti-Social Behaviour Orders. It's possible that introducing the order might have caused more people to report them, rather than more being committed.

2.

Statement: People are more willing to report anti-social behaviour because the Anti-Social Behaviour Order exists.

Answer: Probably True.

Explanation: Since the amount of anti-social behaviour being reported has increased since the order has been introduced, it's likely that the introduction of the order has made people more willing to report anti-social behaviour.

3.

Statement: The amount of anti-social behaviour in the UK has increased since 1998.

Answer: Insufficient data to say whether it is true or false.

Explanation: This might be the case, but it's just as possible that the same amount of anti-social behaviour is being committed, but the amount of it being *reported* has increased.

4.

Statement: The amount of anti-social behaviour has increased every year since 1998.

Answer: Insufficient data to say whether it is true or false.

Explanation: There are no statistics in the passage to even suggest that this is the case. Therefore, we can't conclude whether this statement is true or false.

Section 10 – Deductions

> *Not everyone who owns a car has a driving license, and not everyone who owns a driving license owns a car. Everyone who has a driving license has taken their driving test. However, everyone who drives on the road has a driving license, but might not own a car. Jack drives on the road. Therefore:*

1.

Statement: Jack owns a car.

Answer: Conclusion Does Not Follow.

Explanation: Jack has a driving license, and drives on the road. However, not everyone who drives on the road owns a car. Therefore, it does not follow that Jack owns a car.

2.

Statement: Jack has a driving license.

Answer: Conclusion Follows.

Explanation: Everyone who drives on the road has a driving license. Jack drives on the road. Therefore, Jack has a driving license.

3.

Statement: Jack has taken his driving test.

Answer: Conclusion Follows.

Explanation: Everyone who drives on the road has a driving license. Everyone who has a driving license has taken their driving test. Jack drives on the road. Therefore, Jack has taken his driving test.

4.

Statement: All drivers on the road have taken their driving test.

Answer: Conclusion Follows.

Explanation: All drivers on the road have a driving license. All people with a driving license have taken their driving test. Therefore, all drivers on the road have taken their driving test.

Section 11 – Evaluating Arguments

> *Should it be illegal for individuals working at a company to become whistle-blowers, leaking information to expose perceived injustice?*

1.

Statement: No – companies should be held accountable for breaking the law or being immoral, and the general public has a right to know about this because the behaviour of these companies affects society.

Answer: Strong Argument.

Explanation: This statement argues that, since these companies have an impact on society, then society has a right to be made aware of their wrongdoings.

2.

Statement: Yes – employees leaking information about their employer is no different to a soldier leaking military secrets.

Answer: Weak Argument.

Explanation: This is a false equivalence. In the vast majority of cases, leaking military secrets can put lives at risk, whilst whistle-blowing on companies is far less dangerous. They may be similar in principle, but the severity of one compared to the other is too great to make this a valid comparison.

3.

Statement: Yes – whistle-blowers should be punished but should only receive a suspended sentence or a fine.

Answer: Weak Argument.

Explanation: This is an argument to moderation. Parties both for and against whistle-blowing could be left unsatisfied by this solution, and therefore it isn't necessarily the best one.

Section 12 – Inferences

> *In 2016, a record number of university students appeared at a protest in London against the current government. Recently, the government suggested that they would be raising tuition fees from £9,000 to a higher value. Student unions across the country stated that they would be advocating and organising protests at Westminster if the government suggested raising tuition fees to over £10,000 per year. These unions mobilised for protests in 2016.*

1.

Statement: The government planned to raise tuition fees to over £10,000 per year.

Answer: Definitely True.

Explanation: This is definitely the case because the student unions stated that they would organise protests if the government planned to raise tuition fees to over £10,000 per year. The passage also states that the unions mobilised for protests in 2016. Therefore, the government planned to raise tuition fees to over £10,000 per year.

2.

Statement: Students were protesting because of the proposed rise in tuition fees.

Answer: Probably True.

Explanation: Student unions advocated protests at Westminster for an issue that primarily affects students. It's probably the case that students were protesting for this reason, but it's not guaranteed.

3.

Statement: It is only students that are protesting at Westminster.

Answer: Insufficient data to say whether it is true or false.

Explanation: There's no evidence in the passage to either justify or disprove this claim. Therefore, we cannot know whether it is true or false.

CONCLUSION

Now, you should have everything you need in order to pass the Critical Thinking test. Remember that the test itself is not an assessment of raw knowledge, but of skills. You need to be able to interpret arguments and information, and draw reasonable conclusions from data.

This means that practice is the best way to prepare for the Critical Thinking test. Even if you've already answered all of the practice questions and the sample test in this book, make sure you go back and test yourself again. Make use of the explanations in each of the previous chapters in order to find out where you need to improve.

Also, for any psychometric test, it is helpful to consider the following…

The Three 'P's

1. Preparation. Preparation is key to passing any test; you won't be doing yourself any favours by not taking the time to prepare. Many fail their tests because they did not know what to expect or did not know what their own weaknesses were. Take the time to re-read any areas you may have struggled with. By doing this, you will become familiar with how you will perform on the day of the test.

2. Perseverance. If you set your sights on a goal and stick to it, you are more likely to succeed. Obstacles and setbacks are common when trying to achieve something great, and you shouldn't shy away from them. Instead, face the tougher parts of the test, even if you feel defeated. If you need to, take a break from your work to relax and then return with renewed vigour. If you fail the test, take the time to consider why you failed, gather your strength and try again.

3. Performance. How well you perform will be the result of your preparation and perseverance. Remember to relax when taking the test and try not to panic. Believe in your own abilities, practise as much as you can, and motivate yourself constantly. Nothing is gained without hard work and determination, and this applies to how you perform on the day of the test.

Good luck with the Critical Thinking test. We wish you the best of luck in all of your future endeavours!

GLOSSARY

Glossary of Fallacies

Here, you can find a list of the informal fallacies most likely to appear in the Critical Thinking test. These include definitions and examples. Further explanation can be found in Chapter 4.

Fallacy	Definition
Ad hominem	Personal attacks made by the speaker against their opponent either to distract from the debate or to undermine their credibility. e.g. *'What would you know about the poor? You grew up rich and went to private school!'*
Ad populum/ bandwagon fallacy	An argument or statement which is accepted purely because lots of other people believe it to be true. This is a fallacy because it is entirely possible for all of those people to be incorrect. e.g. *'This musician must be the best ever because they've sold the most records! A hundred million people can't be wrong!'*

Ambiguity	When a conclusion of an argument is derived from unclear premises.
	This is a fallacy because meanings are being confused in order to make an argument more convincing. Often, this is used to cover up a leap in logic, which is unwarranted.
	e.g. *'The dog likes to play. Therefore, the dog likes to play chess.'*
Anecdotal evidence	The use of personal experience or isolated cases, in order to generalise about a larger group of events. This is a logical fallacy, because your personal experience is not a sufficient sample to make generalisations out of.
	e.g. *'Everyone I know who takes drugs doesn't have a job. So, anyone who takes drugs is lazy.'*
Appeal to authority	The claim that, just because some kind of authority says that *X* is true, it must be true. Authorities can include celebrities, politicians, monarchs, and more.
	This is a logical fallacy, because this authority could be wrong like any other ordinary person. What matters is the evidence for a claim, not who made the claim.
	e.g. *'Einstein believed in God, as well as lots of other intelligent people such as Isaac Newton and Charles Darwin. Therefore, it makes sense to believe in God.'*

Appeal to emotion	Trying to evoke an emotional response from either your opponent or the audience in order to make your argument seem more compelling.
	In these cases, the emotional appeal is made *instead* of a rational reason, usually to disguise the fact that the argument isn't founded on logic or evidence.
	e.g. *'Somebody think of the children!'*
Appeal to false authority	Similar to appeal to authority, but in this case the authority is dubious. Either their credibility can be questioned, or their relevance to the areas of debate is uncertain.
	e.g. *'The lead singer of my favourite band supports this party, so I'll be supporting them too.'*
	In some cases, this might be an authority with a vested interest.
	e.g. *'The expert in homeopathy says that it succeeds where conventional medicine does not. Therefore, we should use homeopathy more often.'*

Appeal to nature	An argument which assumes that, just because something is natural, then it must be good. Likewise, things that aren't natural are considered bad. Sometimes, this argument is framed as 'playing God' such as in cases of advanced medicine. This is a fallacy because things that are natural aren't necessarily good, and things that are unnatural aren't necessarily bad. e.g. *'I don't eat genetically-modified foods because they contain chemicals and other unnatural elements.'*
Argument from ignorance	This is the assumption that a claim is true because it is yet to be proven false, or cannot be proven false. Likewise, it is the assumption that a claim is false because it is yet to be proven true, or cannot be proven to be true. This is a fallacy because, just because we don't currently have the evidence to show that something is true or false, this does not automatically mean it is either true or false. e.g. *'There's no evidence to show that God exists. Therefore, God does not exist.'* *'There's no evidence to show that God does not exist. Therefore, God exists.'*

Argument from incredulity	This is sometimes referred to as an appeal to common sense. The speaker makes the claim that, because something seems unlikely, improbable, or ridiculous to them, it is therefore either false or likely to be false. e.g. *'Some people say that humans evolved from apes, who evolved from something more primitive, all the way back to simple life forms. I don't know about you, but I find this to be pretty absurd.'*
Argument from silence	When a conclusion is made because there's no evidence against it, as opposed to making a conclusion with evidence that supports it. e.g. *'There's no evidence to show that we **do** possess free will. Therefore, we **do not** possess free will.'*
Argument to moderation	This fallacy occurs when the speaker assumes that the compromise between two opposed positions is always the correct one. This is a fallacy because it assumes that an 'extreme' position has to be incorrect. However, a compromised middle ground can actually be less preferable than any extreme position. e.g. *'Both the death penalty and rehabilitation are both too extreme. Instead, we should just have capital punishment for the worst crimes, and rehabilitation for everything else.'*

Begging the question	A form of circular reasoning in which the conclusion is included in the premise. Therefore, the conclusion must be accepted in order for the entire argument to be accepted. e.g. *'We can trust the Bible because it is the word of God. The Bible says that God exists. Therefore, God exists.'*
Burden of proof	This occurs when the speaker is responsible to prove their claim, but shifts this onto their opponent to prove them wrong instead. If you are making a claim, then you need to substantiate it with evidence. It is not the job of your opponent to prove your claim is false unless you have sufficient evidence to prove its truth. e.g. *'I believe that the rise in immigration is the cause of increased crime in urban areas. Prove to me that this isn't the case.'*

Cherry-picking/ Texas sharpshooter	This occurs when the speaker picks specific data to suit their argument, therefore trying to make it more convincing.
	This is a fallacy because the sample of data being used to support the argument is not representative of the larger body of statistics.
	e.g. *If someone wanted to prove that a rise in immigration caused higher crime rates, they might only pick areas where the crime rate has increased in order to make a pattern where there isn't one.*
Correlation proves causation/false cause	A statistical fallacy that assumes that if there's a correlation between two or more occurrences, then one must cause the other(s).
	This is a fallacy because it doesn't acknowledge that there might be hidden causes for both occurrences, or even that the correlation is pure coincidence.
	e.g. *'There has been an increase in GCSE grades after the government changed the marking criteria. Therefore, the new marking criteria has improved GCSE grades.'*

'Fallacy' fallacy	This fallacy is made when someone assumes that, just because an argument contains a fallacy, then its conclusion must be false. Rather, it's entirely possible that the conclusion is true, but the way the argument has been formulated is simply faulty. It might be possible to formulate the same argument in a non-fallacious way. e.g. *'Your argument for why healthcare should remain free relies on an appeal to emotion. Therefore, people should have to pay for healthcare.'*
False dichotomy/ black-or-white fallacy	A fallacy which is made when the speaker claims that there are only two distinct sides to an issue. This is a fallacy because it's possible that there are many different stances along a spectrum between these two extremes. e.g. *'If you're not with us, you're against us.'*
False equivalence	A fallacy of inconsistency where two arguments are compared as equal, but in fact they are not. These often appear in cases of politics where a candidate will talk down their own major flaws by highlighting another's minor issues. e.g. *'Yes, I might have hacked the database and stolen people's identities. I'm still better than my opponent, though – he can't even show up to a debate on-time!'*

Gambler's fallacy	The belief that one can go on a 'run' when it comes to statistically independent occurrences, such as dice rolls, roulette wheel spins or coin flips. This is a fallacy because these occurrences are statistically independent. The number that the die lands on in roll 1 has no impact on where it lands in roll 2. e.g. *'I've been on a bit of a losing streak, so I'm definitely due a win on this next spin.'*
Hot-hand fallacy	Similar to the gambler's fallacy, but implies that someone who has been successful in the past with apparently random events will continue to do well. e.g. *'Let her take your money to the roulette table. She's been on a roll, so your best bet is to let her play.'*
Loaded questions	Questions which contain a presumption. In turn, this means that the person being asked the question will look guilty no matter how they answer. This is often used in tandem with an *ad hominem* to force the person being asked the question to go on the defensive. e.g. *'So tell me – do you **still** believe that homosexuality is immoral?'*

No true Scotsman	A form of special pleading where a generalisation is changed to exclude counterexamples, ensuring that the generalisation remains true. e.g. *Speaker A: No Scotsman would drink wine.* *Speaker B: I'm a Scotsman, and I drink wine.* *Speaker A: Well, no **true** Scotsman would drink wine.*
Single cause fallacy	The oversimplification of causal relationships to suggest that there is only one cause of an event. This is a fallacy because it neglects the possibility that there are multiple causes for a single phenomenon. e.g. *'The explanation is simple. Crime has increased over the past few years because immigration has increased.'*
Slippery slope	The belief that a small first step will lead to a chain reaction of events, resulting in an inevitable and unpleasant conclusion. Therefore, this first step should not be taken. This is a fallacy because there's usually no evidence for why the first step would inevitably lead to this later one. e.g. *'If we legalise cannabis, we're opening the door to other drugs being made legal. Eventually, we could end up with even more dangerous drugs being available over the counter.'*

Special pleading/ moving the goalposts	When the speaker makes exceptions to help protect their position when it is proven false. This is a fallacy because it involves changing definitions or creating excuses out of thin air. e.g. *An alternative medicine might be tested under scientific conditions and found to be false. An advocate of this treatment might then say that, in order to work, the medicine has to be done under conditions that weren't in a lab.*
Straw man	A fallacy which is committed when the speaker misrepresents an opposing position, and then creates an argument to attack the misrepresentation. e.g. *Speaker A believes that the prison system should focus on rehabilitation rather than retribution. Speaker B: Speaker A is mad! He wants us to let all of our criminals back onto the streets!*

WANT TO PASS MORE PSYCHOMETRIC TESTS?

CHECK OUT OUR OTHER TESTING GUIDES:

FOR MORE INFORMATION ON OUR TESTING SERIES, PLEASE CHECK OUT THE FOLLOWING:

WWW.HOW2BECOME.COM

Get Access To

FREE

Psychometric

Tests

www.PsychometricTestsOnline.co.uk

20765212R00110

Printed in Poland
by Amazon Fulfillment
Poland Sp. z o.o., Wrocław